Endorsements

"Immediately after reading the chapter by Candace Ellerbe, I thought of people who needed it. Candace masterfully presents not just the problem of debt, but the strategy for getting out of it. What a welcome word! My wife and I are honored to share a cul-de-sac with the Candace and her husband Duane. We have witnessed first-hand their generosity, hospitality and ingenuity. They manage their lives in a fashion that sets an example for us all and, I'm quite sure, puts a smile of the face of their heavenly Father. Thank you, Candace, for your hard work. I'm sharing your message with others!"

Max Lucado, Speaker, Best-Selling Author, and Pastor at Oak Hills Church

Desiree Cook's "A Complete Turnaround" is the kind of story that makes you pause and stand in awe.

Through God's grace she didn't just turn her life around, she spun a full 360 and birthed I Am You 360, a movement that proves beauty, purpose, and power can rise from brokenness. Read this chapter to witness real transformation.

Dr. Tonya R. Strozier, CEO & Founder, Black and Brown Girl Wellness | Ubuntu Academies

Thriving: Making Bold Moves! is a powerful and beautifully written anthology that illuminates the many ways individuals have engaged with money and finances throughout their lives. Through inspiring personal stories, it offers readers both wisdom and practical steps to build wealth one decision, one action, one moment at a time. This insightful collection transcends generations, communities, and financial backgrounds, making it an essential guide for anyone committed to achieving lasting financial literacy, empowerment, growth, and wealth.

Dr. Cheree Meeks, Diversity, Equity, and Inclusion Consultant and Speaker, President, NAACP Tucson Branch

"This book is a powerful motivator that inspires everyone to believe that financial freedom isn't for the select few rather it is attainable for anyone willing to be curious and take action. By sharing their personal journeys and offering practical guidance, the authors empower readers to start where they are to grow their wealth and become the change makers who will impact generations."

Jyrece McClendon, Dean of Academic Affairs, Palm Beach State College

In times of normalized chaos, it's time to shift from survival mode and learn how to THRIVE. This book is a divinely orchestrated blueprint for the times in which we live now. Step into your future and make bold moves. Chanda Allen-Baffoe, shares a masterclass on the path to financial freedom.. It's not as hard as you think. This book will show you how.

Christy Rutherford, Executive Leadership Expert

THRIVING

Making Bold Moves!

DR. AMANDA H. GOODSON

Thriving: Making Bold Moves!
by Dr. Amanda H. Goodson
Featured authors (in alphabetical order): Chanda Allen-Baffoe, Marvin Carolina Jr., Desiree Cook, Candace Ellerbe, Lovely Ganthier, Dr. Amanda H. Goodson, Je're Harmon, and Dakeesha Wright

Editing: Adam Colwell's WriteWorks, LLC, Adam Colwell and Ginger Colwell
Book Design: Gretchen Dorris with Inktobook.com
Published by: Amanda Goodson Global, LLC

Printed in the United States of America
ISBN (Paperback): 978-1-951501-43-3 priced at $19.97
ISBN (eBook): 978-1-951501-44-0 priced at $12.97

Acknowledgements

CHANDA ALLEN-BAFFOE

SPECIAL THANKS TO my parents, whose love laid the foundation—especially my mother, who planted seeds of financial wisdom through hard work and sacrifice. To my husband, whose steady partnership fuels every leap; to my son, whose light fuels my pursuit of purpose and impact; and my godchildren, who add to my "why." To my siblings, friends, mentors, and mentees, who challenge and uplift me. In honor of my God, who has brought me this far and will never leave me. This chapter is a hymn to freedom, stitched with faith, family, and the fire to rise.

MARVIN CAROLINA JR.

I WOULD LIKE to acknowledge and thank my parents, Marvin Senior and Jeanette Carolina, who taught me the foundation of thriving. They nurtured my imagination, protected my dreams, and showed me how to transform bold ideas into real possibilities. To all of my coaches, teachers, mentors, friends, and colleagues, thank you for pouring into me the wisdom, encouragement, and perspective that fuel my ability to thrive and take courageous steps forward. Every lesson, conversation, and challenge has shaped the results you see today. Finally, to my amazing wife, Michelle, thank you for your unwavering love, support, and belief in me. You are my daily reminder that thriving is not just about success— it's about growing together with purpose and gratitude.

DESIREE COOK

I AM GENUINELY grateful to be a part of such an incredible team of co-authors. I want to give thanks to God above all for guiding my past, present, and future. I owe a heartfelt tribute to my Warrior Queen Mom for her strength and the invaluable life lessons she has instilled in me. A special appreciation goes to my husband, Terry Cook, my steadfast support and God's blessing in my life. My heart is filled with love for my seven children, who are my true reflections and gifts from God, as well as my nine grandchildren. I also extend my deepest gratitude and admiration to my mentors. A special tribute to my very first mentor, a true blessing in my life, and seed planter Dr. Amanda Goodson, Kristen Hernandez, Susan Dubow, Nikieia Johnson, Dr. Tonya Strozier, and Arika Wells.

CANDACE ELLERBE

THIS JOURNEY ALONGSIDE such remarkable authors has been both enlightening and inspiring. First and foremost, I give honor to God, who is the head of my life. His grace, guidance, and favor have sustained me every step of the way, and for that, I am profoundly grateful. To my husband, Duane — you have been my boulder since the day we met at Wendy's. Your patience, wisdom, and unwavering support have guided me through twenty-seven years and counting. I am endlessly grateful for your steadfast love and belief in me. A special and heartfelt thank you to my very first client, my beloved grandmother, Edna Mae Carpenter. When all I had was a dream and my own strategy, you trusted me blindly. Thank you for trusting me to help you become debt free at the tender age of 81. I love and miss you from the depth of my soul. To my mother, siblings, uncles, aunts, cousins, nieces, nephews, in-laws, godchildren, and dear friends — thank you for loving me even when I've been persistent about living a debt-free life. The Ellerbe Mantra: "Discipline outweighs motivation."

LOVELY GANTHIER

I AM HONORED to be part of a wonderful group of co-authors and was blessed to have been asked to support this amazing project. Special thanks to my family, friends, and mentors who continue to inspire me to live my purpose.

DR. AMANDA H. GOODSON

I'D LIKE TO thank my family for their continued support in my endeavors to write, speak, train and coach. Along with so many other things that I have the opportunity to be blessed to do. My husband Lonnie, you are such an amazing man, and you are perfect for me. To my son Jelonni, thank you for loving me how I am and allowing me to love you back. To my mom, sister and extended family thank you so very much for being there for me always.

JE'RE HARMON

I WOULD LIKE to express my deepest gratitude to my incredible mentor, Dr. Amanda Goodson. Your leadership, vision, and unwavering encouragement have profoundly shaped my journey and continue to motivate me to pursue excellence and purpose in all that I do. To my amazing parents, Marlon and Lisa Harmon, thank you for your unconditional love, guidance, and belief in me. You have been the foundation of my strength and the source of my determination. To my extended family and dear friends—thank you for your constant support, words of wisdom, and encouragement. Each of you has played a meaningful role in my growth, and I am deeply grateful for your presence in my life.

DAKEESHA WRIGHT

TO MY HUSBAND, whose unwavering love and belief in me make every dream feel possible. To my amazing children, Jaya and Kai—you are my greatest inspiration and the reason I strive for more each day. To my sister Kim, thank you for always standing by me, cheering me on, and reminding me of my strength. To my friend Odetta, who first set me on this journey—your encouragement and faith helped turn vision into reality. And to all my Family and Friends, your collective support has been the heartbeat of this journey.

Table of Contents

INTRODUCTION

Exceed Your Financial Expectations!

DR. AMANDA H. GOODSON

WHEN I WAS a girl in Decatur, Alabama, my younger sister, Yolanda, and I often spent the night at the home of our maternal grandmother, Amanda. A short little lady who loved traveling and playing Bingo, my grandmother lived until she was almost 102. She was an entrepreneur who owned a little community store where she sold homemade Bebops, frozen Kool-Aid in plastic cups, along with potato chips and other snacks. My grandmother displayed perseverance and tenacity. She was not afraid or ashamed of anything, and when I was around her, she always calmed me down if I was frustrated or upset about something. She was feisty in her own way, yet she was also very giving. She just had that spirit around her.

Her home was our Sunday hangout. It was a friendly place with a big fireplace in the living room where we burned coal mixed with wood, and I got an opportunity to stir the fire every now and then when it was cold outside. I had to stand close and very aware because when certain woods popped, hot embers flung onto my clothes and skin. Sometimes, I even got the chance to sleep in that room near the fireplace. My grandmother made us a pallet of blankets on the floor then placed another blanket on top of us. It was cozy, but whatever the accommodations, when I went over for those sleepovers, I thought I was really doing something. It was as though I was a princess with all the riches in the world! That's how it was with my entire family. We may not have had the best houses or greatest of things, but we were wealthy in love.

So, I never really thought about having money, getting wealthy, or being a millionaire. In fact, it wasn't until my junior year in high school that I first realized I needed to decide what I was going to do for a living. My sister and I used to lay in our beds at night, dreaming about that very thing. I asked her, "If you could do anything in life, what would it be?" She said she wanted to travel the world. I then responded, "I want to be on stage." Whether it was as a singer or a musician, I wanted to be a performer and, more broadly, to be up in front of other people. Later, I came to understand that my desire to speak in front of people, to guide and influence them, was a leadership trait, and that is something I have certainly fulfilled as an adult.

At that time, though, my dream had a decidedly entertainment bent to it. However, my dad, Harold, better known as Genie, took another view toward my future.

"The way you like to live," he told me, "you need to make a lot of money."

When he first said that, I wasn't sure what he was talking about. But I did like nice clothes, cars, and houses, and I wanted to go do things that were expensive, at least for us. He then added, "You like to live high on the hog."

Armed with that perspective, I went to the library to research what professions paid well that might fit with two of the interests I'd identified over the years as a student: math and music. It was clear. Engineers and accountants generally made money while musicians didn't. That settled it. I attended Tuskegee University, got a bachelor's degree in electrical engineering, and started working at the National Aeronautics and Space Administration (NASA) close to home at the Marshall Space Flight Center in Huntsville, Alabama. Yet, I still wasn't thinking about having or building wealth. My father had taught me about saving money, but we never talked about investing or anything else beyond that.

Then Jim, one of my new coworkers at Marshall, a man who was direct and truthful to a fault, became a friend. As we got to know one another and discussed our goals and what our futures might hold, he advised, "You could be a millionaire by the time you're forty if you just make some changes."

I didn't believe him. I couldn't even perceive how that could happen.

I never pursued it. I just did my work, and everything was good.

When I stopped working for NASA in 2003 and moved to a different part of the country and a new company, I knew that I needed to assess my financial realities. I was still moderately young when that light bulb turned on. I began working in corporate America and quickly realized that things there were different than they were when I worked with the government. I had-assumed that government retirement would take care of everything, but I saw that there was no way I could retire with that money alone. I had hardly saved any money over my adult life. I hadn't even looked into investing. I didn't have the presence of mind to think about it. I didn't know what I didn't know, so I didn't have a mentality to invest. I had no idea what my net worth was, nor did my husband, Lonnie.

We realized at that point in our lives that he, in general, brought more money to the table through his 401(k), but I had more equity to offer because I'd previously owned a home. At NASA, the government offered thrift savings plans rather than 401(k)s, and I had participated but only minimally. It became clear to me that Lonnie had saved more of his income than I had. Looking long-term, I saw that if I continued doing nothing with the money I earned, he and I wouldn't have enough to live the lifestyle that I wanted to have.

I recalled my father's words and smiled. He was right.

I remembered Jim's bold statement and realized he'd been right, too.

It was high time to change my mindset and my actions.

I examined the time frame Jim had cited, compressed it according to how old I was then, and discovered that I still had time to start saving, investing, and creating wealth to get where I wanted to be. At the same time, I began to take notice of what other people were doing with their money, including individuals I was mentoring professionally as an engineer or personally as a pastor. That caused me to understand that the credit card debt that I had gradually accumulated over the years was another problem I had to address. My credit score was okay, but I had definitely bought stuff that I didn't need, usually because it was on sale. I'd lived true to the flawed adage, "If it's on sale and you don't need it, it's not a sale." I admitted that I had done exactly what retailers wanted me to do: buy, buy, buy and spend, spend, spend.

Those realizations birthed a steely resolve within me.

"I can say 'no!' I can stop buying those things."

So, Lonnie and I got started. We began catching up where we were behind and saving and investing extra as we could. We were not doing some things and going without others. It wasn't terrible. We did fine adjusting to a new way of thinking and managing our money. We determined what we needed to make and save monthly to have everything we required over the course of a full year. We limited trips. We didn't eat the same way. When I bought something, clothing for example, I saw it as an investment. I paid a little more for better quality, but I'm still wearing most of those outfits today. We managed the pretax and after tax funds that were invested in our 401(k)s. I didn't always put in the maximum amount. Sometimes I only put in what was required to get the matching funds benefit from my employer. Lonnie and I had separate bank accounts, and whatever was left after all of our expenses were placed in mutual funds. We learned, we adapted, and we remained consistent.

Twenty years later, in 2023, I launched Bold. Millionaire.Women (BMW) with the conviction that women need financial literacy so that they can build wealth for themselves, their children, and their families. I devoured books on financial literacy and wealth and saw gaps that I could fill, particularly in my community, to help women take the lid off of how they think and see themselves in relation to money.

The movement grew and gained momentum to the point that I hosted the first annual BMW Tucson Takeover conference in the fall of 2024. Several of the authors in *Thriving: Making Bold Moves* attended that conference at the Pima Community College downtown campus in Tucson, Arizona. We had a packed house, and it was overwhelmingly successful. Over and over, attendees told me, "I did not know that," or "Thank you for doing this," or "My husband needs to hear about this." The prevailing sentiment was, "Please continue to do this because it has made a difference in my life!"

The conference provided opportunities for mentorship and coaching, and those who came went to work on changing the way they saved and invested money. They were excited to get on it right away, and they have maintained that momentum. Everyone from young people in their twenties to folks in their sixties attended. We had Gen Z, Gen Y, Gen X, and Baby Boomers all in the same room, and each one of them got something out of it. There were people who were arriving not-quite millionaires who talked about how they had grown from making five figures to six figures and were striving toward seven figures. There were others who were already millionaires and multimillionaires who talked about their path to wealth and financial freedom. A panel of best-selling authors focused on how to have the mindset of a person who can become successful and grow. One precious attendee, who was close to 70 years of age, asked if it was too late, and she learned that it was not too late—for her or for anyone else.

BMW started with women, but between feedback from the ladies who said their husbands needed to learn these principles and the men themselves who said they wanted to come, I expanded BMW to include men via the

Bold.Millionaire.Women Plus Men Academy. Everything we do at BMW is designed to raise and heighten expectations, awareness, and financial acumen—to flip the coin from being a person who is a borrower to a person who is a lender and one who is able to have both active and passive income. One of our biggest messages is how building wealth and creating financial freedom can not only cause all of us to live a fuller life but also give us the incredible ability to leave a legacy.

"It's not just about you," I tell my BMW family through my monthly webinars. "It's about what you are doing to infuse the culture with a Kingdom language under the financial umbrella and make a difference for the community and for your family long term. You need to make a path for your kids, grandkids, and great grandkids, so they have longevity and opportunity. You can have a fund that helps them pay for college. If you don't have kids, you might have nieces and nephews or people in the community who you gravitate to that can benefit from you."

We are changing the way people see finance and wealth. Arriving millionaires are being inspired to continue to move forward and head toward thriving millionaire status. Thriving millionaires are being inspired to continue to thrive while lifting up arriving millionaires. *Thriving: Making Bold Moves* will share a few amazing stories like those that will interest, engage, and inspire you!

In Chapter 1, Candace Ellerbe will show you how to "Take Control" of your finances with discipline and determination, while in Chapter 2, Desiree Cook will inspire you with how her life became "A Complete Turnaround" so that she can now help others in need.

In Chapter 3, Je're Harmon tells you about the "Audacious Moves" she's made to grow and develop her wealth before I return in Chapter 4 to help you "See the Possibilities!"

In Chapter 5, Lovely Ganthier shares some unique insights about her journey toward financial independence that is both encouaging, enabling, and very "Well Done." In Chapter 6, Dakeesha Wright inspires you to go to "Even Greater" heights in your pursuit of wealth. Then, in Chapter 7, Chanda Allen-Baffoe details her "Journey to Financial Independence" before Chapter 8 concludes with Marvin Carolina Jr. sharing the "Risky Business" he's achieved to gain and maintain all that he has earned and learned.

As you read *Thriving: Making Bold Moves*, it is my hope that you will have an open mind and be ready to develop a wealth strategy that will far exceed your expectations, outlive you, and create a compelling future for people around you that you may never meet this side of eternity. You can make a tremendous difference as you pursue and gain your financial freedom!

Dr. Amanda H. Goodson
Founder and President
Bold.Millionaire.Women™

CHAPTER 1

Take Control

CANDACE ELLERBE

IT WAS IN the wee hours of the morning when a fearful revelation compelled me to want—no, to need—to become debt free so that I could have financial freedom.

Today, over two decades later, I'm an Information Technology (IT) program manager for Platinum Technologies, a major tech company in Virginia. Platinum Technologies is contracted out to the United States Department of Commerce, I manage a team of several people, and we work with customers to ensure goods are imported and exported from other countries to and from the U.S. I work remotely from my home in San Antonio, Texas. I am still married to the love of my life, my husband, Duane, who retired in 2020 after 26 years of service in the U.S. Air Force.

But back on that fateful morning on Tuesday, November 30, 2004, we lived in Hampton, Virginia, my husband was a staff sergeant at Langley Air Force base—and I was working as a systems analyst at CACI International after six months of unemployment following the loss of my first job as a production planner at Newport News Shipbuilding. With the benefits I'd received while out of work combined with Duane's income, we were paying all of our bills on time. In fact, we had just bought our first home. Duane got the mortgage loan in his name, and I was on the title and deed with him. I was so thankful for our home and happy to be in it.

But we were in debt, living paycheck to paycheck—and it was during that half-year that I was unemployed that I made a promise to myself.

If God gets me out of this, I am going to get out of debt. I don't want to go through the stress of this again.

It was 3:30 a.m., and I couldn't sleep. I was downstairs on the sofa in the family room with a blanket draped over me watching television, the only light in the room coming off the screen, when it suddenly dawned on me.

If something unexpected or catastrophic happened to the home or otherwise, I couldn't help us.

I was making great money. So was he. But we had no savings. We both had loving families, but they didn't have any extra money.

No one could save us.

Heart racing and adrenaline surging, I hurried up the stairs, darted into our bedroom, and woke up my slumbering husband. I shook his shoulder, and he jumped out of bed and leaned over to turn on the lamp on the nightstand. "What's wrong?" he screamed.

My husband has beautiful light brown eyes, and they came wide open from the shock of me waking him up. Being military and startled from sleep, he probably thought someone was in the house.

"Listen," I blurted. "We've got to get out of debt! We are broke!"

Duane was stunned. The initial look on his face strongly suggested that he wanted to kill me, but I guess he saw the worry in my eyes because his expression instantly relaxed—and I'll never forget what he said next.

"Okay. So, what do you want to do about it?"

Abruptly aware of what I'd just done and what time it was, I quietly replied, "We'll talk about it when you wake up."

"I *am* up," Duane said calmly, and he hugged me. I could still feel his heart racing from being awakened so abruptly. "Let's talk about it now."

Wearing shorts and a shirt, he walked downstairs with me. We turned on the overhead light and the chandelier directly over the kitchen table and sat down to begin our discussion. There were no preliminaries. We just dove into it.

"Where do you want to start?" Duane asked.

"Let's get our credit report," I replied.

That was the first time we'd ever pulled it up. My credit score was 518. His was 702. It was clear my credit was already shot and that had to change, while his debt to credit ratio was high because he bought the house by himself. Now we can easily download an application and see our credit history every day. Technology has sure evolved.

Next, we wrote down all our debts, including everybody we owed and where we were delinquent. Although each one of us brought one debt into our marriage that was mine and his alone, we treated those as our debts. In my view, there are no separate finances in a marriage. We signed up to be in it together all the way, for richer or for poorer. So, we took the "poor" parts and rolled with them as a couple. We wrote down how much income we brought into the home. Within minutes, we were able to clearly see what was going on.

I looked at the numbers. "Do you think you can pay every bill in this house for a year with just your income?" I asked.

He said he could.

"Then I'm going to get us out of credit card debt next year."

"Okay," he replied, smiling. "If I'm going to be responsible for every bill in the house, then you need to come up with a plan for how you will stay on track to pay off the debt."

That was when I created a plan and my first spreadsheet with formulas and calculations for all the bills and amount I was going to pay on each one. I filled in the cells and columns with data, and off I went! Today, over 20 years later, I still use that same spreadsheet.

Duane and I were on a mission.

Our journey toward becoming debt free was underway.

To be honest, I didn't know how we were going to be able to do it. I just knew we had to. Actually, I knew we were going to do it, but I didn't think it would happen all that quickly. I was determined. I started by putting myself on a $100 budget every two weeks. That was used to put gas in the car and to cover basic self-care, getting my nails done ($13.00) and my hair taken care of ($20.00). That was 2004, so $100 was enough to get those things done back then. The rest of my income was directly allocated to pay off debt: credit cards, two car loans, my medical bills from before we were married, student loans, and personal loans. I employed the snowball method, listing all the debts from lowest to highest. Five of those debts were delinquent, so I tackled them first, and I gained valuable insight as I dealt with them. Whenever I called a creditor or collection agency about a delinquent bill, I discovered that I needed to be ready to pay. For example, one of them was for a credit card that I'd acquired in college. It only had a $1,000 limit when I got it, but I owed about five times that because of the interest that had accrued.

"I'll give you one thousand dollars today," I said.

There was a brief pause. "Please hold on," the representative said, and the elevator music commenced.

I waited until she returned. "Could you give us two thousand?" she inquired.

"No," I replied evenly, "but I can give you one thousand right now."

I heard, "Please hold," and the tune started again.

She got back on the line. "How would you like to pay the thousand today?"

"Every two weeks, you can have three hundred thirty-three dollars, and on the third two-week period, you can have three hundred thirty-four." I then read off the account number, routing number, and three check numbers, post-dated for those amounts, and that was how I paid them off. I didn't have to pay any of the interest accrued.

Truth is, very few people are paying off delinquent debt. Therefore, creditors or collection agencies will take whatever you give them, assuming it is a fair offer. They exist to collect anything they can, so make a deal, and 98 percent of the time, they'll take 20 to 30 cents on the dollar to settle the account. If someone is going to give them *something*, they're more than happy to receive it.

I stayed the course, month after month. I spent my $100 and used the rest to pay debt. When it was all said and done, the value of all of those debts was about $25,000, excluding our mortgage and my student and car loans. That was a lot of money for us.

But by three days before Christmas 2005—just over one calendar year later—that debt was gone!

Duane and I were relieved, but we didn't do anything to celebrate our massive achievement. Instead, we set right to work on the next set of debt: Duane's car loan totaled $35,000, my car loan totaled $20,000, and my student loans came in at $26,000. Our home was $176,000. I continued paying monthly on those, and we literally started throwing money into our savings account. Every dime we got that didn't need to be used for a monthly expense went into it. As we were doing this, my husband was on his third deployment, so for the six months at a time that he was overseas, all of the money he earned was tax free.

In 2009, when he got orders to leave Virginia and be reassigned in Mississippi, I again found myself unemployed because of the move. Life was good, though, because when the housing market crashed in 2008, we were able to put a contract on the house in two weeks and walked away with a 27 percent profit. Every penny went into savings. It took me six months to find another job—but all the while, we stayed the course and trusted God to provide a way out of the situation. I collected a severance from my previous job since my manager was able to lay me off before the move rather than have me resign. I also received an unemployment check from Virginia until, in January 2010, I was hired at a digital patient engagement technology company as a test engineer in Mobile, Alabama, a one-hour trek away from our home in Ocean Springs, Mississippi. We took as much of my income as possible and fed the savings account. This was hard, especially considering that I took a 23 percent pay cut going between different regions. I had to stay disciplined because sometimes things didn't stay on the trajectory I thought they were supposed to go. Still, by the end of 2012, we paid off Duane's car. We had sold the house in Virgina and were renting in Mississippi.

We'd been amazingly self-controlled, but then I undermined things with an emotionally-driven decision. Duane was again away on his seventh deployment to Virginia, and I was in a very unhappy work situation in Alabama. When I visited my husband in Virginia for Thanksgiving, I convinced him to let me visit a car salesperson I'd worked with in the past. Two of my friends had just purchased beautiful cars, and I figured a new vehicle of my own would help me feel better. I traded in my perfectly reasonable car for a shiny new 2012 Acura RDX right off the showroom floor. They shipped it to Mississippi, and everything was great—until the vehicle arrived at my home. I instantly had buyer's remorse as I realized I had set us back in our goal to become debt free. I knew I had messed up. Yes, I had a new beautiful car, but I had to roll over the balance to the new car loan. Basically, it was like starting all over when I was almost finished. It was frustrating, but I immediately moved forward.

When Duane got orders to move from Mississippi to Tucson, Arizona in 2013, we bought a house within a month of arrival there. That left us with a $210,000 mortgage, the $40,000 car loan on my Acura, and the remaining balance on my student loans, $26,000. Up to that point, I'd paid the minimum each month, but the interest ate away at any possibility of gaining ground on decreasing the overall balance owed. So, we developed a new budget plan to clear up the car and student loan debts. At the same time, we had been working on starting a family in Mississippi with no results. After we relocated to Arizona, we learned that in vitro fertilization (IVF) was our best option. However, Duane's military insurance didn't cover the procedure, so we had to decide how to finance the $11,000 cost. Would we use existing funds from our savings account or get another loan?

Growing up poor, I couldn't imagine that much money leaving our account at one time, but we knew we didn't want to thwart our debt free journey. We took the plunge and paid out of our savings account. It didn't hurt our budget plan at all, and we focused only on car debt first. Then we hit the big ticket items like the student loans. After two years of IVF (five rounds of embryo transfers), we were still unsuccessful in having a child. Duane was on his twelfth deployment, and we kept paying on our debt and stacking away money like it was the end of the world. All of Duane's deployments were not easy on me, but I stayed faithful and consistent to the plan. We weren't perfect. There were emergencies and interruptions that we had to take care of. One time I thought, *We have to dip into our savings to purchase a new roof. However, it isn't so bad because that's what savings is* for. Life was happening. We'd set goals and start making progress, then something would happen or we'd decide something was important and we needed to do it. Those things had an effect. We were finally able to rationalize going on a vacation. We hadn't been on one since 2008.

Yet every time we got paid, we were throwing our money at a debt.

Then, one morning in summer of 2016, Duane and I were brushing our teeth when I told him without warning, "Hey, I'm paying the student loan and car loan off tomorrow." There was still $12,000 left on the student loans and $10,000 to go on the car.

"Are you sure?" he asked. I could almost hear him thinking, *You're giving them all that money?* But I was done. I was over it. Those were the last two bills. We could have paid them off by the end of that year, but I didn't want to wait.

"Yep."

"Okaaay," he replied, drawing the word out like he still just wasn't too sure about it.

I didn't pay them off right that minute. I had to let the idea set in for a few hours, a carryover of my poverty mentality from childhood. I took one last moment looking at the account, with all of that money in it, before making the payments—then I just pulled the plug and did it within five minutes.

We had $235 left in the one savings account we'd set aside for those loans. We still had another savings account being funded as a six month emergency fund.

I know a lot of people would've seen that number and asked, "What have I just done?" But I wasn't scared. I was relieved. I never struggled with it. I knew that by the end of the year I would get it back in there somehow. That was the mentality switch that informed my decision and my attitude about that decision. What was left in the account was not important. The important thing was that the debt was gone, whatever its amount.

My god sister once told me she owed $200 dollars to a tire company. "Do you have the two hundred dollars?" I asked her. She said she did. "Then give them the money," I directed.

"That'll only leave me with twenty dollars," she replied, and I could hear the anxiety in her voice.

"I know but remember—you'll get paid again in a week or two. Pay off the tire company, and you won't have to worry about that bill anymore. It's not like you're waiting for a miracle. Another paycheck is coming."

A positive, realistic mindset goes a long way, and Duane and I certainly had that going for us once we were finally free of consumer debt. Only our mortgage remained, but because we knew we'd be moving one more time, we weren't immediately concerned about selling the home. That happened later in October 2021. The housing market was booming, and we were able to sell the home we bought in 2014 at a 92.8 percent *increase* over what we originally paid for it.

We were in shock. It was wonderful, and we had made it!

We were completely debt free!

In late 2024, I served on the thriving millionaire panel at the first annual BMW conference in Arizona. I shared with the ladies how, before I'd even heard of Dave Ramsey or Suzi Orman, Duane and I came up with our plan to be debt free and have financial freedom. Through it, I understood how much money was coming in and how much was going out. I listed four categories in a computerized spreadsheet. The first was every-day expenses such as bills: the mortgage, gas, water, electricity, and food. The second category was enter-tainment; basically, things we wasted money on: going out to eat, nails and hair, shopping including shoes, and vacations. The third column was delinquent bills. Then, in the last one, I listed all of our debts that had an inter-est rate from the smallest to the highest. I did it in that order because I needed confirmation that when I paid off something, it was working. I felt like I was winning, and it gave me motivation to keep going.

It was so simplistic. I made my lists. I was honest with myself. Then I figured out how to do it.

Being honest with yourself is the hardest part about managing your money. It can be very intimidating. Many people have ignored the reality of their situation and are barely getting by. When you sit down to look at your credit report and see what and who you owe, it may scare the socks off of you. But I wasn't scared because I was so mad! I was angry that I had gotten myself in so deep. I felt irresponsible because I knew better. I was upset because I had chosen to be ignorant.

The crazy thing is that it has come full circle. When we first started in 2004, it was all about me getting out of debt. I didn't want to be in a situation where I was unemployed and worried about owing so much money. When I was able to tell Duane that we were debt free and he retired from the military after working 26 years to protect our country, he didn't have to go to work again until he was ready. COVID-19 happened just weeks after Duane retired, and he was able to take the rest of the year off while I kept working!

I had no idea how much my husband would benefit from us being debt free. I had always looked at it as, "I'm not stable. I might lose my job. I don't want Duane to bear the burden of paying bills because we don't have enough money coming in." 2020 turned out to be our best financial year! We banked so much money because we didn't go anywhere. Then, in January 2021, Duane got a great job offer to run an Amazon Web Services (AWS) data center in San Antonio, Texas.

Today, Duane and I live on two acres in a 4,100 square foot home in Texas. We are on a mission to pay off that home by 2035.

People who know me know that I've always hated buying water bottles. I feel like water should be free. It is a natural resource from the earth. Therefore, I also despised paying the water bill, and I'd insist that I was going to find a way to get rid of my water bill someday. Of course, it was just a running joke. I had no idea what I was talking about, but nevertheless, today I have no water bill because we have our own well. It's pretty amazing!

Two young ladies reached out to me right after the BMW conference. One has paid off four credit cards since October 2024. Another is a married mother of two and a teacher. I shared how people don't realize how much they spend for groceries. She said, "Candace, I took your advice, and we cut back on our grocery bill." She now saves over $200 a month at the store.

It's simple discipline, isn't it? Oftentimes, the reason we are not meeting our goals and, therefore, are not thriving and excelling is because we lack self-restraint. I believe God blesses obedience. If you lack discipline, how are you going to be blessed? Those two don't go hand in hand. It's no surprise. That's the biblical design. That's why the minute I get off track, I can tell, and I can reel myself back in. God looks for the change of heart that results in a change of behavior. That's when we begin the process of becoming more like Him.

Of course, discipline requires self-control. I am an avid shopper who works from home. I love shopping, but every day I have to control myself because it's so easy with the internet. It is right there in front of me. All I have to do is push the button. Even as I wrote this, I was keeping myself from contacting my sales associate at Gucci to send me this cardigan I've been wanting. Let me tell you, the battle is real! Sometimes it's the hardest thing, especially when I tell myself that if I fall off the wagon, I can get right back on. My conscience is the key. I pride myself on integrity. That's what keeps me grounded. I have a personal core value about spending money correctly that I take seriously, and I hold myself accountable.

Mentors can really help in this or other areas of personal or professional development. While I currently don't have a financial mentor to provide knowledge outside of what I'm already cultivating as a Bold Millionaire Woman, my business mentor, the amazing Patrice Waters, has molded me into the leader I am today. I have learned self-awareness from her, and she has taught me that I don't have to attend every fight I am invited to. I need to carefully pick my battles. Because of what I've developed through Patrice's tutelage, executives have placed me into positions where I am able to excel. I am very grateful for that. Patrice has also served as my sponsor, going to others and declaring, "Candace can do this." The Chief Executive Officer at Platinum Technologies, Jermon Bafaty, sees something in me (as crazy as I am). He admitted that he sometimes gets nervous when I need to speak to a group because he doesn't know what I am going to say, but he respects me. He values my input. More than that, he values me as a person. I also have an advocate in Jermon. I can go to him with a specific need, and he'll say, "Let's discuss." He challenges me to convince him of the need. He has the power to place you in rooms that will help you excel. I attended the McKinsey Black Leadership Program, where I discovered that a mentor teaches us how to speak on our own while an advocate will speak on our behalf, and a sponsor will make it happen for us.

This type of interaction with others is so fulfilling. It just makes me feel good because I come from humble beginnings. My mother had me at 18. My grandparents started raising me permanently when I was four. It was during that time when a child could be raised by a grandparent without any legal ramifications. When my grandfather passed, their children were grown and had their own families, so it was just me and grandma. We were poor. She raised me off of $375 a month with no state assistance until I was in ninth grade. She was my biggest supporter, and it makes my heart burst to know that I helped her get out of debt when she was 81 years old.

He left quite a legacy for me to follow—and when I look back at the little girl I was back then, there's no way in the world I would've dreamed I'd be where I am today.

I see three simple strategies as being the most effective for creating and building wealth. The first one, that is brought out time and again in my story, is discipline. Second, you have to determine where your project plan is derived from, so list everything: your debts, your income, your expenses, and your investments. Don't be shy when you do it. A lot of people get discouraged when it comes to debt because they don't want to face how much they owe. Facing your debt and your fears could be the hardest thing you'll ever have to do in your life. It is very intimidating. It hurts, and it's scary. But in order for you to plan effectively to succeed, you have to know what you are working with. Finally, you need to make a plan and execute it. You can go at it randomly or willy-nilly if you want, and you'll likely fail doing it that way. A plan gets it done—and guess what? Those numbers get a little less scary every time you see your progress toward eliminating debt. They're no longer some giant beast that can't be slayed. You can eat away at it, little by little, until you get there. That was really encouraging to me, and I saw that I could do it! Grandma used to tell me, "Fear and faith can't reside in the same place within your head. Choose faith, and walk in it."

As I continue to understand and manage my wealth responsibly, I never stop learning. I continue to read and follow financiers, listen to podcasts, or read books on money. The Bible encourages us in Proverbs 3:5-6 to not lean on our own understanding, and I don't. What I do understand may not be fully correct or enough, so I listen to other people who are wealthy to discover what they do differently with their finances and then think about how I can execute those things with my own finances. That empowers me to become a willing risk taker and see what outcomes I can achieve. For example, a neighbor once sat with Duane and I after a homeowners' association meeting and said he wanted us to get together with his financial advisor so that we could start investing in the S&P 500 (Standard & Poor's 500) stock market index. It tracks the performance of 500 of the largest publicly traded companies in the United States and is widely regarded as a key indicator of the health of the U.S. economy. When people drop nuggets like that, you can investigate them further to see if they're right for you. Watching opportunities cat-apult into something great is amazing!

Strangely, investments did not play any role in our strategy to build generational wealth until 2021. Our plan was to be debt free, not to become millionaires. Since 2004, we have eliminated debt and saved money. That was all we did. Yet our savings had certainly grown. Spurred by the sale of our first home in 2009, Duane started an IRA account in 2010 while I began mine in 2016 after we paid off the student loans. We both contribute 20 percent of our income to our retire-ment. By the time Duane retired in 2020, we had a sub-stantial amount in our savings account. But we weren't privy to anything else. We didn't have anyone around us who was investment savvy. The very first person who talked about investments was my grandma. She paid for my wedding reception by selling a certificate of deposit (CD), a type of savings account that pays a fixed interest rate on your deposit for an agreed-upon period. For all I knew then, a CD was a compact disc. The second person who told me that I needed to invest was Dr. Amanda Goodson. We happened to be talking at the beauty shop, I shared what was in my account, and she declared, "Oh, you need to move that!"

"And do what with it?" I asked.

She gave me different ideas on what I could do to move my money, and Duane and I began looking into investments. During a hard freeze in the early winter of 2023, Duane and I were under a blanket watching television, a cup of hot chocolate in my hand. Duane got an alert on his phone about an email from American Express. They were offering a money market account earning 5.25 percent. At that moment, we moved money over to take advantage of that deal. The bank we moved the money from immediately called and asked if everything was alright. I said, "No, we aren't making money with you, so we are moving our money." Money market shares came next as Duane earned some of the shares through his job for Amazon Web Services and participated in the purchasing of others. Then we increased our allotment to our 401(k) accounts, and they skyrocketed. Finally, a good friend and real estate entrepreneur, Nicky Isaac, who wrote the book, *The Millionaire's Blueprint*, started coaching us into purchasing two investment properties by the end of 2025.

Our goddaughter, LaDasia Bush, a real estate agent, kept us informed on the market and what areas were best to purchase.

I'm constantly attentive to balancing my desires versus my needs as I continue to grow my wealth and practice financial responsibility. I still like to shop; however, I'm very strategic with what I spend my money on. I am not frivolous with it. The vast majority of the time, I get the things I desire on sale. I stay disciplined by remembering how it felt to owe someone. I don't want to go back there. I find the role of credit in wealth management to be quite interesting. I have a friend who is a millionaire and totally into using credit. I am not into credit at all. Credit reminds me of how I got into financial trouble to begin with. I didn't understand it; therefore, I abused it. Duane and I don't have anything on credit other than our home mortgage, but we do have one charge card. The difference between a credit card and a charge card is that a credit card charges interest. With a charge card, you just pay your balance at the end of the month. To me, the charge card suits my needs better because it stays in the realm of self-discipline, whereas a credit card allows me to become irresponsible.

It may be just me, but I've concluded that credit is not needed to become wealthy, no more so than investments are needed to get out of debt. Those are lessons I've learned from my own experiences. I tell people all the time regarding getting out of debt, "You have already played with your money. You've got to get serious about this. Now is the time to buckle down." For so many people, their money troubles are the result of having a good time and living beyond their means. I add, "You don't have any options when you are in debt."

Your only option is to get out of it.

When you do, you are free to do some incredible things. One of the proudest moments in my life was being able to educate my grandmother on how to become debt free at the age of 81. Born in 1931 during the Great Depression, her mother cleaned white families' homes and her grandmother, who partially raised her, was blind. So, my grandmother understood at a young age what hard work was. When she became an adult and married my grandfather at age 18, she was primarily a homemaker while he worked a civil service job. She was a great influence as she helped navigate raising her four children—and after I was born, she began raising me alone when I was eight after my grandfather passed away at age 54.

My grandfather passed away at age 54, and she was left with a small monthly annuity stipend from his retirement benefits with the Department of Defense. She was able to pay her house off soon after his death using a life insurance payout, but the annuity was barely enough to cover utilities, groceries, and necessities.

I recall my grandmother keeping a ledger for years, writing her bills on the left, the payment in the middle, and the balance on the right. I believe that's where my spreadsheet idea came from. No matter what the circumstances, she always paid her bills on time, amazing when you consider that 54 percent of America's lower class fall into credit card debt. It becomes survival of the fittest to provide for a family using credit because the interest rate eats away at the debt, keeps chewing, and never seems to spit you out.

So, it was 2014 when my grandmother called me about a debt consolidation program. I was curious about how the program worked and called to get more information. I learned that they were able to contact credit companies and work with them to reduce payments and cancel interest. When I asked how they did that if lenders didn't agree, I discovered that their tactic is to make huge payments to the highest debt and stop paying the others. I didn't like that because that would make her delinquent on some payments, and I was concerned that it would negatively impact her credit score. However, as I thought about it, I realized that she was 78 and owned her home and car. She didn't need her credit.

Since I only had knowledge about how to deal with delinquent credit, I wasn't sure how I was going to maneuver this plan, and all her creditors were current. So, I discussed the process with the company. I wanted to be involved with their technique when it concerned my grandmother's financial well-being. I was leery of scammers. I'd heard horror stories of the elderly losing everything. I continually thank God that my grandmother trusted me and was wise enough to say, "Let me run this by Candace."

I told them how, if and only if we agreed to their terms, I felt responsible for overseeing any decisions made regarding her credit and finances. The song and dance went on for three months before my grandmother and I agreed to let them represent her. Her representative and I decided on a monthly payment feasible for her, and he assured us debt would be paid off in three years.

She paid them off six months earlier than that. We were so excited, and the only thing she had to pay after that were her utilities. It was amazing.

The legacy I hope to leave in terms of wealth and values is simple: self-discipline. People don't realize how blessed they will be if they are just disciplined and obedient. The Bible says that God will bless you when you are obedient, and if part of that blessing is not having people calling or texting you every two minutes to get their money, that's peace of mind. I know too many people who are threatened by not having enough money.

As I finished writing this chapter in the summer of 2025, I was on furlough from my job. While on furlough, I lost my grandmother at the sweet young age of 93. She lived a long life well fit for a queen. Even more, she died debt free. As executor of her estate, the only bills I had to resolve were for water, electricity, and the internet. Her home was paid off and gifted to me, and it became our very first investment property. That is what financial freedom looks like—and I pray that everyone can transition just like she did. Kudos to you, "Suga!"

Because Duane and I managed our money and created wealth, I did not blink during my furlough and was in a great position when it ended and I returned to work. I am good. I am living life. I am very relaxed. I am not stressed. All my bills are paid.

I love this quote from Dave Ramsey. He says, "Live like no one else, so you can live like no one else." Live like no one else today, so when it is all said and done, you can live like no one else later. Take control—and you will know the peace of mind that financial freedom brings.

Candace Ellerbe is an accomplished Program Manager with over two decades of experience leading IT initiatives in support of government contracts. A seasoned leader in the Computer Science sector, Candace is known for her ability to streamline operations, drive policy compliance, and develop high-performing teams through strategic coaching and mentorship. Her leadership style balances firmness with grace, earning her a reputation as a respected and trusted leader.

Candace's expertise spans test engineering, Agile and DevOps methodologies, and cross-sector IT operations within both Federal and private industry environments. She is committed to delivering results, implementing best practices, and fostering innovation across platforms and teams.

Recognized as a Women of Color Technology All-Star Award recipient, Candace's contributions to innovation and thought leadership have been nationally celebrated. She is also a graduate of the McKinsey Academy's Management Accelerator Program for Black Leaders, further enhancing her executive management and strategic growth capabilities.

Contact Candace at candycaneconsulting@gmail.com

CHAPTER 2

A Complete Turnaround

DESIREE COOK

THOSE WHO KNOW all that I have been through and all that I am still learning today may find it hard to believe that I was raised in relative privilege in an upper middle-class family. Born in Newark, New Jersey and raised in nearby Plainfield, I was able to travel the world (Canada, Spain, Morocco, Jamaica) and enjoy the finer things (horseback riding, the best restaurants and clothing) thanks to my father, Charles, an entrepreneur whose success gave us a comfortable life. In fact, I come from an entrepreneurial family. My grandfather and relatives on my mother's side were also prosperous business owners.

Yet despite all those advantages, I learned nothing about finances growing up, and I certainly didn't do any better as a young woman. Frankly, I still have a lot to learn today—even if I have now worked to raise over $2 million through my nonprofit organization, I Am You 360, to build affordable, energy-efficient, and environmentally friendly tiny homes for aged-out foster or unhoused people aged 18-22 in Tucson, Arizona. Called the Small Home Experience, we cut the ribbon to launch construction on the first of those homes on December 3, 2024.

How I got to where I am from where I was is quite a story. At I Am You 360, we believe that we all have a story to tell, and when we start to share our truth, not only is it freeing, but we also see the commonalities we share with each other. We understand that, "You know what? I am you," therefore we can help each other make a complete turnaround, a 360, for the better.

God knows that's what I had to do—and my narrative and the truth it shares proves how surprising my accomplishments truly are.

I had a great relationship with my dad. He was my king, my hero, a good man, and a great father and husband. But I was 17 years old when pancreatic cancer took my father away from me. It was quick, all within three months after a surgery to address digestive issues revealed Stage Four cancer that was too far gone to do much anything about. He did chemotherapy treatments at home. My dad had always been a strong man, someone who really commanded his atmosphere, yet I recall being downstairs watching *I Love Lucy* and hearing him angrily yell, "What are you laughing at?" The cancer was spreading, and he was in so much pain. He got to the point where he wouldn't eat, and he didn't want anyone to see how frail he was.

A few days before his death, my grandmother visited us and asked me to take her to a church to pray. I did, and by the time we came back, my mother, Gert, was getting my father dressed. He wasn't breathing right, and an ambulance was on its way. Dad was admitted to the hospital, and I remember sleeping with my mom that night. When we went to see him the next morning, the prognosis was dire, and I began making phone calls to let others know that he was about to pass. I returned to his bedside in intensive care, and his heartbeat went down so quickly it was horrific. I had a fit and had to be removed because I was so disruptive. I eventually calmed down enough to be let back in to see him—and as life ebbed out my father's body, I leaned down to him and whispered, "Daddy, I feel like I just died, too."

At that moment, I became the same as a walking dead person.

The words we speak to ourselves and others are powerful, for good or for bad.

After the loss of my father, my life fell apart. My self-esteem went downhill. I began looking for love and attention to fill the void of missing my father. Within months of his death, I became pregnant, and I had my second child by the time I was 19. Where I was from, the fast life was common. I knew about the streets, as much as my parents tried to shield me from them. So, it was easy to get into the fast life and stay there. At that time, crack cocaine was an easy way to make money, and I put myself out there to sell drugs.

Soon after I started dealing, I tried crack with my childhood best friend, and I liked the way it made me feel. It was euphoric and took me out of my present mindset mentally and emotionally to another place. Considered an upper, it kept me moving around and busy, and it numbed the pain I still embodied from seeing my father take his last breath. I ended up in Brooklyn, New York, and my situation snowballed from selling and using crack to using alcohol, pills, and heroin. During my addictions, my first two children, both daughters, ended up living with my mother, and I had four more kids who were eventually removed and placed into foster care. Of those six kids, I was really a mother to none.

Inevitably, still mired in my addictions, I called my mother, who by then was living in Phoenix, Arizona, and declared, "I am ready to turn my life around." Being who she is, she immediately left her home, came to Plainfield where I was renting a room with the latest man in my life, and took me back home with her. It was time. I was sick and tired of being sick and tired, and my mother, my Warrior Queen, rescued me. That's when my long journey out of the abyss began. Patiently, my mom helped me kick my addictions. Under her care, I first went through about six weeks of terrifying withdrawals. It was horrible. My daughters would peek through the door and stare, and I saw the hate, embarrassment, and shame in their eyes. They were surely thinking, "What can you do for me? I want nothing to do with you."

Lovingly, my mother nursed me back to health, and I got a job in the cosmetics department of a JC Penney. Dressing nice for work and serving customers really helped my self-esteem, and it was the first time in my adult life that I learned to build relationships without having an ulterior motive. When I was able to rent my own apartment, though, mom wisely felt she should keep my two daughters with her until I was really ready to take care of them myself. My girls didn't like me, and that was really stinky. My second oldest daughter had a lot of hate toward me that she would carry for years. Kids teased my daughters about being raised by their grandmother and having a mother who was an addict. Those burdens and the toxicity they caused affected both girls. Then, eight weeks after I got the apartment, my mom received a call from back east stating that my other four children would be placed for adoption if my mother couldn't take them in. That's when my mom selflessly went from housing two of my children to taking care of all six of them.

I'd been given an incredible new chance at life, including a job upgrade from JC Penney to the communications company MCI where I was an in-bound call representative. But I nearly destroyed it. A year later,

I relapsed and began living a double life of addiction and maintaining a relationship with my mom and children. But what's done in the dark will come to light. My addiction eventually got so bad that I started lying to my children about why I didn't pick them up from school or answer their phone calls. Then, one day, I simply disappeared. I stopped going to work and began living on the streets on the west side of Phoenix. My life became getting high, coming down, and doing it over again—all day every day. I was so embarrassed that I'd let my mom and my children down again. Getting high helped me numb my own pain, even as I caused pain to the very ones that loved me the most. I got arrested a few times and did a couple of months in the Maricopa County Jail. I was released from my last stint in the county jail on the condition that I get a weekly urine analysis, but after a few weeks I would no longer comply. I was arrested once more for drug possession, and at age 32, I was sentenced to three years in prison starting in 1999.

I was incarcerated in three different prisons during that time, the last one being in Tucson, and it certainly wasn't easy—but it actually saved my life. Serving time gave me the opportunity to pause and get reacquainted with Desiree and all that my parents had tried to instill but that she had let fall to the wayside.

It was a turning point, the start of my 360, and I determined that I was going to leave prison better than the way I went in. Near the end of my time, I became eligible to do a work furlough. I worked and went back to prison at night. I saved my money, and when I was released from prison April 1, 2002. I got my own apartment. Three weeks later, I met Terry Cook, the man who would become my husband. We got married that August, rented a house together, and I've never looked back.

My next mission was to get my children back. We got my eight-year-old son first toward the end of 2002, and in 2003 we got my second youngest daughter, age nine. I had another daughter with my husband at around the same time. The following summer, I got custody of my 11- and 12-year-old daughters, and all of the children I'd originally lost to foster care were back with me. My oldest daughters, who were raised by my mom, were still unhappy with me, and they opted to stay in Phoenix with my mother, but today, I'm happy to say I have an amazing relationship with them.

Once I had my children, it was all about being present and healing. I was there for them when they woke up and when they went to bed. I made breakfast on the weekends and listened to their stories. We had a lot of family activities in the backyard and built some great memories together. My kids were active in sports, so my husband and I went to all of their games. It was amazing to see my kids blossom and be happy. In Terry, they had a dad who was their protector, and I was learning how to be a mother, wife, and citizen in the community. I had to learn to forgive myself, and my children had to learn to forgive me.

All along the way, I wasn't perfect, but I was discovering how to love myself. I rose to the occasion, and I am grateful to God for giving me the resilience, the maturity, and the critical thinking and problem-solving ability to do so. At one stage, I had four kids in high school all at the same time, and they all graduated. It was amazing.

I went from being a mother to none to a being mother to all of them. Today, I have been married for 23 years, and I have an amazing relationship with all seven of my children, which is priceless. I even have nine grandchildren.

I have been brought 360, full circle.

God gave me the vision for what I am doing today with I Am You 360 as I was positioned to see clearly what was going on in the community around me and noticed how the already-existing foster care crisis was increasing. There was a disheveled look about the kids in foster care. Foster care parents are obligated to ensure the children under their care look well-kept and are treated as valuable individuals, but I didn't see it in my community, and I wanted to do something about it.

I was a hair stylist and firmly believed that just because someone was in the foster care system didn't mean they had to look unkempt or unwanted.

Society considered the foster care population to be throwaways. They were the forgotten ones, and they often looked that way. My desire was to provide a full hygiene program to meet their needs and give them the tools to change their outward appearance. That would in turn help to transform how they felt about themselves inwardly.

It started in my living room. I called a local foster care group home and told them I wanted to provide hygiene for their clients, and the officials there were nice enough to give me the ethnicities of the girls currently under their care. I contacted some friends, and we went to work! We had "pack the bag" parties where we prepared hygiene bags according to the age and ethnicity of the girls at the group home. We delivered them on Martin Luther King Day, 2014. At first, the girls, ages 14-18, were standoffish toward us. But once they started looking in their bags, I could see the lightbulb go off. Their whole energy changed. All of a sudden, they saw us as allies. It was an amazing transformation. I Am You 360 was born.

Since then, we have served over 5,000 youth and families through I Am You 360. We refill the hygiene bags every six weeks. That consistency improves the appearance of our clients, from when they are very young all the way into their young adult years. It also improves self-esteem. It improves school attendance and academic success. It combats bullying. Good, basic hygiene is something most people take for granted, so for years many folks didn't understand the importance of the bags and the program. But when the COVID-19 pandemic hit and the Centers for Disease Control and Prevention emphasized things such as washing hands, a new respect for hygiene arrived. It turned out we were ahead of the curve. As a society, we hear talk about housing and food insecurity, but we don't ever hear anything about hygiene insecurity. Yet there is a reason the health and beauty industry is a bazillion dollar business and there are rows and rows of health and beauty products at the store.

Using strategic, forward thinking and progressive concepts, we created the movement I Am Somebody in 2018. We developed a curriculum that is focused on self-love, self-awareness, and positive thinking. Kids of trauma need self-love. We help retrain the brain in a fun, interactive setting. Next, I was given the additional assignment to start a housing program after a generous donor gave I Am You 360 a 10-unit complex with studio-sized living spaces. From there, it took three years to raise the nearly $2 million required from donations and grants for the project, and we found a contractor who allowed us to pay as we went. Every other contractor wanted all of the funds raised up front.

At the start of 2025, I Am You 360 continues to grow as an award-winning nonprofit organization with the goal of empowering the whole person. Our home ownership program allows us to steadily place funds into escrow for our clients so that they can purchase their first starter home after three years. We are actively advocating for underserved populations in our community with folks in the foster care system and the unhoused as our primary target groups. Finally, we provide life skills classes for residents covering everything from cooking and cleaning to financial literacy, banking, and credit management.

As my clients learn, I am learning with them. It's amazing to realize that my pursuit of proper money management and generational wealth has been birthed out of a passion to help others following a life of addiction and destruction. Now, as I oversee my nonprofit organization, I am developing the knowledge and mindset to tend to my own financial freedom as well as that of my family. My mother moved to Tucson during the COVID-19 pandemic, and I wanted to be able to help her financially. I'm putting money aside, learning what compound interest and high yield banking are, and taking classes through the Bold Millionaire Woman program. The financial and credit reputation of I Am You 360 is amazing, and I want to mirror that with my personal money management and wealth creation. I want to have better credit. I also want to have at least three months' income saved and to be able to cover all of my mother's rent, as well as having investment properties. I also wish to start a college fund for my grandkids. That's why I'm an *arriving* millionaire. I am building all of those skill sets and applying what I've learned with my nonprofit to make my personal goals happen!

Three mentors are aiding me in this endeavor. I met Dr. Amanda Goodson in the salon, one of my colleagues did her hair she would listen, advise and guide me while I was still creating I Am You 360. She always challenged me, "What are you going to do, Des, to be different? What are you going to do to be sustainable?" Another lady, Susan helps me with the challenge of problem solving. She gives it to me straight and helps me brainstorm and come out with a clear understanding of what I need to do. Finally, Harriet has taken me under her wing and speaks life to me. She checks me if I need to be checked. I am also mentoring my Small Home Experience residents. So many people have done a disservice to them. I build trust with them, and it is so fulfilling to see my mentees receive guidance that they ultimately embody and apply. To see their eyes light up and watch them blossom is priceless.

When it comes to creating and building wealth, I truly believe that first and foremost you need to build a personal relationship with *self* so you can learn and understand your strengths and weaknesses. It is less about taking a strategic look at investing in stocks and bonds and that kind of thing and more about your mindset and positioning yourself for success. Once you have done that, then you need to embody resilience and determination to finish what you start.

A Complete Turnaround: Desiree Cook

A lot of people have amazing ideas on wealth and millionaire-ship, so to speak, but the foundation they are working from is not firm. If I've learned anything from creating new homes for my clients, it's that the foundation has to be solid in order to build on it. That's what I am doing in my life. I am building out from the firm mental foundation I've established, and now I am ready to start doing what needs to be done to create other streams of income to arrive at millionaire-ship. I was introduced to the finer things in life as a child, and that birthed within me the importance of leaving my children with experiences and resources they can enjoy and learn from. Those things supplement the more significant life lessons I can give them and help position them to succeed and pursue financial freedom for themselves.

I'm just learning how to approach understanding and managing wealth responsibly. The classes I've taken as a Bold Millionaire Woman are allowing me to develop and grow. A fire of knowledge has ignited within me, and I am applying what I have learned to my day-to-day life. I know what is attainable, and I have a personal excitement to arrive there. I no longer doubt it can happen. I can already see it. Being optimistic and viewing finance and wealth through a clear lens is very helpful for my mindset and lifestyle. It makes me more conscious of how I spend every dollar, so I ask myself if something is a need or a want? I'm saving money, and at the same time, I'm learning about the importance of credit. Having a good line of credit says a lot about your character and reputation, so my goal was to have a personal credit score above 700 by the fall of 2025. My next long-term ambition was to look at investing. I know it's not just about me. If I want my biological kids, as well as the youngsters we serve in the I Am You 360 program, to be better than me, then I must learn alongside them so I can educate them.

I Am You 360's Small Home Experience is helping to sow aged out foster kids and their families back into the fabric of the community and doing it with humanity and dignity. It is all intentional and by design. My goal is to become a national and international consultant for other movements to create luxury, affordable, energy-efficient tiny homes. The bar has been raised as we dismantle the old concept of temporary 160-square foot safe housing with what we're pioneering for underserved populations and setting them up for success rather than failure. As all of this happens, generational wealth is being created.

Whether you are just starting out on your road to financial freedom or have been traveling it for a while, be patient with yourself. Sometimes we expect things to happen quicker than normal. Take baby steps. Start small—and stay focused. Write down your important financial goals. That is important. I follow the biblical principle from Habakkuk 2:2 to write it down and make it plain. Yet as you put pen to paper, don't forget to speak your goals aloud. That brings forth manifestation and fruition. Every day, I proclaim, "I am somebody" in the mirror. I am my biggest cheerleader. You have to be as well.

As your wealth builds, I recommend that you do it silently. My mom always told me to never let your right hand know what your left hand is doing. Everybody needs something or wants something, so make your financial freedom happen without openly sharing or being braggadocious about it. You can encourage, guide, and give advice to others about money without ever sharing dollar amounts. Your wealth building journey should be one of your best kept secrets. What's yours is yours. It's private.

What legacy do I hope to leave for future generations both in terms of values and wealth? My father used to say, "Once you die, that is when you have made a name for yourself." Character is everything. What people say about you after you have passed is very important. I want to leave with an honorable reputation and honorable character for my children's children, holding them to a different light to not only fill my shoes, but to walk in them and do a better job than me. Monetarily, I believe in setting them up for greatness as best I can and in such a way that they would want to do the same for their children's children.

Desiree Cook took her lived experiences of drug addiction, 2 children raised by her Mother, 4 children placed in foster care, survivor of domestic violence, and 3 years in prison. She a Mother to 6 but a Mother to none. Upon her release in 2002 she soon got married to Terry Cook and immediately started to get her children to start the healing process to build a healthy relationship and now a Mother of 7 children.

Desiree identified a gap within the community amongst children in foster care and wanted to advocate with a large spotlight on their unique needs to close barriers and gaps within society. With this deep hearted passion she started I Am You 360 in her living room in 2014 a forward thinking, innovative, award winning nonprofit with National attention that focuses on children in foster care or unhoused that provides customized services to boost self-esteem, self-worth, self-love a movement called "I Am Somebody" by providing new, full size hygiene according to age gander and ethnicity refills every 6 weeks, developed a self-focus curriculum to help create whole healed people, and the first African American Woman build Arizona's first energy efficient, affordable tiny home community for aged out foster care and unhoused 18-22 coupled with life skills and homeownership to break generational cycles.

Contact Desiree at iamyou360@hotmail.com

CHAPTER 3

$\diamond$

Audacious Moves

JE'RE HARMON

AS I WAS growing up in Milwaukee, Wisconsin, learning how to save and manage money wasn't a topic we talked about in my middle-class family. I knew I needed money to live and take care of my responsibilities, but anything beyond working and paying bills was something I really wasn't aware of. It just wasn't in my mindset.

As a young kid, I always had the money I earned from my allowance or received as a gift spent before I even got it. At first, I bought everything from candy and food to music and electronics, and as I got older, I bought clothing and shoes. I shopped at the mall often and bought stuff online about every couple of weeks. They were all materialistic things focused on meeting my immediate needs and providing instant gratification. Saving and planning for the future never crossed my mind.

I started college right after graduating high school in 2008 with a 4.0 grade point average. The straight A's had come easily. I was pretty smart with a decent study ethic, but higher education turned out to be a lot harder than I thought it was going to be. I had a full scholarship for all four years, but I had to maintain a 3.5 grade point average each year to keep it, and I never did. Still, they gave me opportunity after opportunity, and my scholarship was renewed the first two years despite my grades. But halfway through my junior year I had to withdraw when my grades prompted school officials to tell me to take a break and get myself together.

That's when, as I returned home and started working as an inventory auditor for major retail stores, I quickly discovered that I still had the same mindset that I did during my upbringing. I needed money to live and take care of responsibilities, so I was cool with simply working to make money. I was living at home, so all of my income was mine. I didn't really have any bills I had to pay. I was excited to work, earn money, and spend it on what I wanted.

Before I knew it, I was getting ready to turn 26 and realized I would no longer be allowed to stay on my parents' health insurance. I was working part time and doing well enough, but I wasn't earning enough to carry the cost of my own insurance. Saving, investing, or retirement never entered into my thinking.

That's when my mentor, Dr. Amanda Goodson, said something that catapulted me on the path to becoming what I am today, an arriving millionaire. It couldn't have been any more simple or straightforward.

"You need to have a job with benefits."

I began looking for jobs with benefits that were in line with my skill set, primarily administrative positions. Dr. Goodson suggested, "Maybe you should look for something in security, not necessarily physical security, but personnel security." That was an audacious move for me, but sure enough, three months later, I applied and was hired for a position in personnel security. My duties included completing applications to obtain work clearances on contracts while maintaining metrics and dashboards using data analytics to help vet people to see if they were trustworthy to perform the duties our company requires. It was a good contract job with good pay, but it didn't come with benefits at first. Within three months, though, things changed when they decided to make my role a full-time position. Not only did I have my own health insurance, but I was able to invest in a 401(k) and a Roth IRA through my employer. From that moment forward, my mindset about my finances shifted. It was no longer just about living and taking care of responsibilities. I realized that what I did with my money would impact where I wanted to go in the future!

When I first started working part time in 2014, I was making about eight dollars an hour. Eleven years later in 2025, I am making $52 an hour. In that span, I also returned to school, earning a bachelor's degree at Northern Arizona University in interdisciplinary studies with an emphasis on humanities and then obtaining a master's degree in business administration from the University of Illinois. Because of those degrees, I have been able to excel and grow within the organization where I work.

None of this would've happened without a change in mindset or mentors like Dr. Goodson who were thriving at a completely different level that I could aspire to reach. It wasn't easy. A huge obstacle that presented itself came in 2020 with the COVID-19 pandemic. Suddenly, my employer wasn't making as much money as it normally made because people weren't doing what they normally did, and I had to take a temporary ten percent pay cut. I had moved into my own apartment at an introductory rate, but that period had passed, and my rent had just increased. That meant my expenses were going up while my income was going down, and I had to figure out how to make that work.

My faith as a Christian is very important to me, and my mentor reminded me that God was the One who paid my rent and who would give me what I needed—and guess what? The entire time I was in that situation, I never missed a rent check. How? God allowed me to make resources in other ways that I didn't even know were possible, such as helping my church to stream its services on the internet. I recorded sermons, put together videos, and sent out virtual invitations to make up the difference in my income. When others told me that once the company took my pay, they would never give it back, I declared to myself that I was going to get my pay back. The following year not only was 10 percent of my pay returned, but I also received an increase in compensation!

Another audacious move that really elevated me to a place of thriving financially was beginning to monetarily give. When I first entered the workforce, I knew that I was supposed to tithe (donate at least ten percent of my income) to my church. But as someone with a limited mindset, I thought, *If I give God this money, that means less money for me.* So, I gave here and there five dollars one week, ten dollars the next, but I wasn't consistent, and I wasn't truly tithing. It wasn't until my thinking changed that I understood that when I tithe and give to God, that creates a financial stream that opens doors for me that wouldn't have opened otherwise.

There is a blessing in tithing. In the natural, it looked like I was giving away money, but I was actually sowing something that would bless me in return. It was all about obedience to God. When I got serious about tithing, I started giving more than ten percent, I saw an increase, and I got promotion on top of promotion. My mindset and my prayers were transformed. It was no longer, "Lord, give me a bonus," but "Lord, increase my tithes!" It shifted from, "Give me money," to "I want to be able to give the church this amount in my tithe alone, plus an offering." I was convinced that if my giving increased, so would my net income—and it did! God has given me a giver's heart. If I see someone in need and I have it and can give without it being detrimental to me, I am open to it as long as it will do good for the recipient as well as myself. I think, *Is this going to benefit them or hurt them? Is this going to benefit me or hurt me?* Sometimes I have to take the emotion out of the decision and be okay with whatever path I choose to take.

Audacious moves such as the ones I've learned to make and maintain required me to confront and vanquish my fears. Whenever I was in that natural, analytical mindset of, "One plus one equals two, so if I don't have enough money, how am I going to do this?" or "If I give this amount of money, I have less. How am I going to pay my bills?" I was feeding my fears. It did not make sense. It felt like I was losing. But when I tapped into my faith and fixed my mindset. I realized that I was not losing. God was going to take what I gave Him—my resources, my time, my energy—and multiply it in different ways so that, in the end, I'd win!

I am victorious, or as I like to put it, "I am on the up versus the down."

As of early 2024, I have purchased a brand-new home. I work from home as a Personnel Clearance Data Analytics Lead at a Fortune 200 technology company, so it gives me plenty of room to both work and relax. I am growing in my professional roles and expanding my career. I am a traveler at heart, too, and I was able to go with my family on a six country tour of Europe in 2023. We started in London, England and then went to France, Germany, Switzerland, Belgium, and the Netherlands. That was a graduation gift from my parents after earning my master's degree. The following year, I traveled to the United Kingdom, and I loved Scotland. I remain busy serving in church and helping to grow the ministry there. God is really doing some great things, and it's been awesome!

Another incredible opportunity came in early 2025 when I took a class through my employer called Transformational Leadership. It taught me about coaching. I lead a team of seven people, so I have been investing in them and doing some career coaching to see where they want to go, whether that is inside or outside of the organization. I ask them to describe where they see themselves in the next two to five years, then have them work backward from there to identify what they need to do to close the gap between the two so that when the opportunity presents itself, they will be capable of stepping into that place. That's the whole point of thriving and making audacious moves. When you get to a certain point, you don't look back. Instead, you help someone else get to where you are and on track to where they want to be.

As you can tell from my story, the biggest thing is mindset. If you have a negative attitude toward wealth, then you will always find yourself not having enough money or being in debt, so you won't be able to do what you want to do financially. But if you have a positive mindset toward wealth, you will do whatever it takes to see your financial goals come to fruition. You will make sure you save what you need to save and that you are not spending what you shouldn't spend. You will make sure you pay your bills on time, which reflects well on your credit score. A part of my mindset focuses on turning a want into a need. For example, retirement is still decades away for me. Most people my age assume they won't retire for an extended period of time, so they don't need to start worrying about saving and investing for retirement until they get closer to it. But I shifted my mindset so that even at the age of 35 I knew I needed to start investing for my future. To make those audacious moves now, I had to shift saving and investing for retirement from a want to a need. That way, I won't need to make huge moves or take bigger risks as my retirement age draws closer.

I've learned that tracking your finances is essential to understanding and managing your money responsibly.

If you don't know where your money is going, you have no way of knowing if you are doing a good job managing it. Someone once told me something profound. "Je're," she said, "you need to give your money an assignment!" Therefore, every dollar that comes to me has an assignment, whether that is paying a utility, investing, or saving. Every single time I get paid, I know where my money is going and for what purpose. Then I can track it to see if I am spending too much in one area or if I should save a little more in another. In addition to giving my money an assignment, I operate by a simple rule. "Can I pay for it in cash?" If there is something I want or desire, it is best to pay for it with cash on hand versus a credit card. This prevents me from over-using credit, and it disciplines me to save for the item so that I can get it in the future. Delayed gratification is an incredibly useful practice that will reward you down the line.

As an arriving millionaire, I believe it is important to have at least seven streams of active or passive income. I have multiple investments. My job allows me to invest in a 401(k) as well as in a Roth IRA, but I also invest in things like cryptocurrency. In addition, today's technology has allowed me to invest in real estate without even having to buy property. I use an app where I put money in, it invests it in different properties and transactions, and I reap the benefits. I continually educate myself on other investment opportunities and weigh the cost versus the benefit, so I can see how much I can dedicate toward a particular investment at any given time. I see tithing at least 10 percent of my income to my church as a stream, as is the money taken from my pay for social security. To date, I have saved a lot of money in my Roth IRA, and I've learned that it is important to max that out every year because it is a pretax investment, meaning that when I do come to the age when I can withdraw from it, I won't have to pay additional taxes on it.

Credit plays a huge role in wealth management. Simply put, a good credit score gives you opportunities that you wouldn't have with a bad credit score. A good score allows you to gain access to more money in terms of loans and investments than you could with a bad score. When I took out my student loans then stopped going to school, the lenders wanted me to pay that money back right away. That was "out of sight, out of mind" for me. I didn't think about it, but in actuality, my credit score was plummeting even as my debt was increasing. So, I prioritized paying off those loans. Another thing I did to improve my credit score to prepare for buying my house is that I bought a car. Then I paid for my vehicle every month on time. My payments were never late, and when I could I paid more than the minimum. I paid it off in five years. As I did, my credit score steadily rose. As of this writing, my credit score sits at a healthy 720.

When I consider investing versus saving, I find that the difference between the two is the timeframe and the return. With investment, you can realize a greater return than you can with savings, but investment money is put away for a longer period of time. Your savings are made up of funds you may need tomorrow or next week, but investment funds may not be needed for years or decades. It is important to know the difference because you don't want to put money into an investment and then pull it out quickly. If you do, it will not reach the capacity that was intended for it. I like the good old saying, "Never put all of your eggs in one basket." Diversifying your money in good investments fulfills that saying. If all of your money is invested in the stock market and it crashes, it's gone. If you put it all in cryptocurrency and that crashes, it's gone. So, if you have a little bit of both and something happens to one or the other, you'll still stay ahead of the game.

In the end, being audacious is all about the small steps. Everyone wants to go from zero to a million in the blink of an eye, but it starts with saving $50 every month or every paycheck and investing it into a good account that will grow interest. Being audacious is all about knowledge. As a part of Bold.Millionaire.Women, I attended its inaugural annual conference as well as monthly webinars that talk about different aspects of wealth. You have to put yourself around people who have already done what you are looking to accomplish and glean from their insights and experiences. Educate yourself from those who know.

I resonate with the story from another one of this book's authors, Candace Ellerbe, and how she steadily and consistently, over the course of several years, worked with her husband to get out of debt so that they could achieve financial freedom. It inspired me to realize that sometimes you just have to dig in. Yes, you want to enjoy life. Yes, you want to do some good things, but you need to focus on your goals to get there. When I was younger, my parents had me go through Dave Ramsey's Financial Peace program. One thing he said that stuck with me is, "If you live like no one else, later you can live like no one else." That means you can't do what everyone else is doing. You can't spend money the way everyone else spends it. You need to build a better future for yourself, so you can have the life you want to have later.

In terms of wealth, I have definitely grown from the mindset that I had as a youngster to the perspective I have now. I had some hiccups along the way, but I'm in a steady place. For those who are coming up behind me, I want to impress upon them the importance of finances at a young age, so they can understand the value of money and of saving, investing, and giving. They don't have to be in debt. That doesn't have to be part of their story. Finally, knowledge is power. The more you know, the more you are able to understand certain things and make certain decisions, the more you can accomplish! Find someone who has been there and done that and glean from them.

Je're Harmon is originally from Milwaukee, Wisconsin, and is an Amazon Bestselling Author of Women Leading by Faith: Make a Difference Now. Now residing in Tucson, Arizona, Je're is known for her infectious laughter, vibrant energy, and genuinely positive spirit. People are naturally drawn to her warmth and enthusiasm.

Professionally, Je're serves as a Personnel Clearance Data Analyst and Logistics Lead for a major aerospace and defense company. She also brings her passion for innovation and collaboration to her role as Vice President of Logistics and Operations for AGG, LLC, where she integrates her love for technology, planning, and facilitation to build lasting partnerships across business, industry, and nonprofit sectors.

Beyond her professional endeavors, Je're aspires to help others grow through media arts and vision casting, inspiring purpose and clarity in those she serves. She credits her success to God's grace, favor, and divine guidance. In her spare time, Je're enjoys traveling and spending quality time with family and friends. Her ultimate mission is to continually expand her influence and capabilities to advance the Kingdom on Earth.

Contact Je're at harmon.jere@gmail.com

CHAPTER 4

See the Possibilities!

DR. AMANDA H. GOODSON

WHEN I ARRIVED in Tucson, Arizona in 2003 after a long career as an engineer at NASA where I participated in some form or another in over 60 Space Shuttle launches, over half of those as Director of Safety and Mission Assurance, it was a massive transition. I was in a brand-new place, and it was far different than I had ever known. I was working in a new position for a new company. I was also embarking on a journey that would see me launch a platform for leaders and entrepreneurs, as well as become the pastor of a church. As told in Chapter 6 of my book *Astronomical Leadership*, it was a challenging and humbling season of my life— punctuated by the realization that my husband, Lonnie, and I had to get to work managing our finances.

The idea of building wealth wasn't new to me at that stage, but it also wasn't something that I naturally understood. I came from meager beginnings. I grew up in Decatur, Alabama in a small, rented house with three very small bedrooms (one of which my sister, Yolanda, and I shared) and a single bathroom. My mother, Mable, worked until my father, Harold, graduated from college when I was three. After that, she stayed at home, while he served in the United States Army as an engineer. Whenever my mom, my sister, and I stayed with my Grandmother Amanda while dad was away on military assignments, I thought it was great, even if I had to sleep on the floor.

My parents, therefore, didn't really start making or accumulating money in any significant way until dad's military career progressed. When they did, it wasn't about getting rich, but more an expectation that we would never be in need. Another expectation was that I would succeed in school, go to college, and get a career where I could make good money. By the time I was in high school, I still didn't really understand wealth because I hadn't seen or experienced it. It was at Tuskegee University where I started to recognize the difference between poverty and wealth, but my view remained incomplete and limited. The concept that a wise person builds wealth in part to leave a financial legacy for their children and grandchildren had not yet occurred to me.

I graduated Tuskegee with a bachelor's degree in electrical engineering, and of the four employment offers waiting for me, I took the one that would keep me closest to home: NASA. I was hired in June 1983 as a professional engineering intern in the test and evaluation branch at the Marshall Space Flight Center in Huntsville, Alabama. My annual salary at that time was around $20,000. By the time I departed from NASA, I accepted a new job and began earning seven-and-a-half times that salary. Lonnie and I had saved or invested some of our shared income, but it was clear we needed to do more.

That's when I thought back to my parents. My father was very frugal, and didn't believe in living in the lap of luxury. When he passed away from heart failure he left resources to my mom that included some bonds he had purchased. He hadn't done anything with those bonds, and my mom didn't know anything about them, but there was enough there that she was able to get a car. He had also invested in real estate, and he owned several houses that he rented out. My mother and I didn't know if he bought those homes as long-term investments. It was likely more as a passive income source to help the family. My mom soon found out that dad didn't always cash the checks when people paid their rent. He was a giver, and that was one of his ways of giving back. He was even involved with the area Boys & Girls Club as a board member. He was a community-based man.

My father had woven all of that into the fiber of our family without me even realizing it. He was working to make things better for his family because we had done without for so long, and my mother benefited from his caring diligence in managing their money.

So, I began to learn. I knew about short-term equity but not long-term investing. Through a 401(k), my employer contributed a percentage of what I put into it, and I could save up to so much money per year. I decided to max it out and get the maximum benefit from them. That way not only was I going to save and have equity, but I was going to invest and have a long-term strategy. Then I decided we were going to double the amount we paid for our house payments each month. I'd heard that if someone pays just one extra payment a year, the mortgage can be paid in full in 20 years versus 30. I wanted us to do better than that. I started saying, "We need to stack more. We need to do more."

I realized that I didn't want to get involved with real estate like my father had. I appreciated what he had done for his family and for others as a landlord, but I saw that as being too much for me to take on. However, I did embrace a new way of thinking and managing my money, and I changed my mindset in the process. I imagined my husband and I being in a different place, and I wrote myself a contract with affirmations about what I wanted to do. I decided what kind of house I wanted and where I wanted to be. My employment had me at times in Los Angeles, California, and I took pictures of the mansions in Beverly Hills and put them on my wall. When movie stars put their homes up for sale, I looked up the specs and started defining what

I liked in a home. I drew a literal diagram with text, an iteration of a design that I wanted of a 6,500 square foot house with six bedrooms and five baths, and then I told myself how much money we would need to have that. I started listening to other people's conversations about finances and asking more intelligent questions about money.

As I made that mindset change, supported with visual aids and affirmations that I spoke aloud and called into existence, doubts would sometimes enter in. Come on, Amanda. You'll never get that. But I countered that voice. "I might as well try. It won't hurt to try." It was all a part of the process, and I took an optimistic view. Lonnie, who takes a more practical approach to things, contributed by asking clarifying "what if" questions that prompted me to think more deeply and clearly. My journey toward financial freedom was gaining momentum, and I was enjoying the ride.

Entrepreneurship played a big part in helping me further pursue financial freedom. When I started my first company, In Focus Consulting and Seminars, in 1993, it was in part to fulfill my longtime desire to be on stage speaking, coaching, and training. That was my way of doing it through the back door. I'd done those things before as a hobby or a side gig, but I'd never made money from it. Through that company, I began learning how to earn income through a platform, and I eventually signed contracts to speak, teach, or coach with municipal and corporate entities. It grew and grew.

The spring of 2014, I became a John Maxwell certified coach and started a second company, Amanda Goodson LLC, which became Amanda Goodson Global as I chose to write the script toward having an international reach. These efforts apart from my day job as an engineer empowered my money management by causing me to stretch. I discovered that I really did not have a global mindset at first, but that developed as I leveraged earnings from my engineering career to stack, save, and invest my finances. I also found opportunities for Amanda Goodson Global to grow. In January 2019, I published *Astronomical Leadership*, the story of my journey from becoming an engineer to moving into entrepreneurship with a leadership-focused platform to further elevate myself and my brand. It became the first of many more books to follow about leadership topics. Some were anthologies featuring insights from colleagues that lifted up their expertise and brought more awareness and growth to Amanda Goodson Global.

In the meantime, the COVID-19 pandemic birthed a new challenge to my thinking about my finances and the future. *I'm still not maximizing my potential,* I thought. *What if something happens, and I don't have a job. How am I going to proceed?* Right before the pandemic hit, leadership at the company where I worked realized that people were going to be home because of everything going on, and my boss asked me if I'd like to work from home. I agreed, I left that day, and I haven't returned to working at a traditional office since. In that time, about four supervisors came and went, and in the midst of COVID, one suggested that I could lose my position as an engineer entirely. But I wasn't flustered. I had already calculated what I needed to earn to meet all of my needs if I was out of a job, so Lonnie and I adjusted. We maxed out employer-provided investments. We paid more on the house to get more equity. If we had extra funds, we paid an additional house payment or put it into another savings account where it could sit and build interest.

Then, after the pandemic, I attended an annual summer retreat for executives at Martha's Vineyard. Cosponsored by Beta Iota Boulé in partnership with The Executive Leadership Council and McKinsey & Company, it is open only to those who are Chief Executive Officers or one step away from being CEO. My longtime friend and colleague (and one of the featured authors in this book), Marvin Carolina Jr., got an invitation for me to attend. My eyes were opened at the retreat. Experts shared about global economic analytics, future jobs in the service sectors, and opportunities in sustainable industries. I learned what kind of background and degrees our children and grandchildren need to pursue to be ready for the years 2050 or 2070. It was amazing!

At the Martha's Vineyard event, I also saw people who had become multi-multimillionaires, something I hoped to achieve. I looked at them and wanted to say, "Where you guys been?" One lady oversaw a bank. Another gentleman, Bernard Tyson, used to run a major health company. He started talking about how he had a heart problem, and he flew all these surgeons in to take care of him on his private jet. I was in awe. I had never heard of anything like that before! Here I was, a grown woman who had never known or understood that so many people had such status!

At that time, I was doing pretty good—but I wasn't where they were.

I thought, *I have to go back and sharpen those pencils.*

I shared everything with Lonnie. "We still are not doing what we need to do," I told him.

"You are saving real deep," he reminded me.

"Yeah, but all of this is available," I declared.

From there, we continued moving forward using biblical principles as our standard. I tithed to the church and seeded into all kinds of things where God promised to give back. It worked. The church was being seeded into and invested in, and it worked. My contracts and investments started growing. As we did things God's way, everything worked. I don't want to mislead anyone. We had to work hard. I discovered that if I had $100 and someone asked me for a dollar, that was easy. If I had $100 and someone needed $90, that was harder to let go of. But if I had $1,000 and someone needed $90, that was easier to give.

That's how God works: for the greater good, for the longest period of time, to maximize the support and help to more people. The more I have, the more I am able to give, to invest, to save, and to do. The wealthy succeed because they don't let money control them. They are in control of their money. They are solution-based people who weigh the ramifications of their decisions, focus on the forces that work in their favor, and understand the factors that can come against them.

Here are nine achievable ways you can develop a wealthy mindset, most of which are drawn from the book and workbook *Financial Healing from the Inside Out* I co-authored with Angela C. Preston

1. **Believe that you deserve wealth.** If you don't believe this, you will sabotage your efforts. Wanting to attract wealth but not believing you deserve it is like trying to drive a car while pressing both the accelerator and the brake at the same time. It will get you nowhere.

2. **Develop an "opportunity consciousness."** Look around and begin to ask yourself, "How can I add more value or solve a particular problem—and make money while doing it?" The bigger the problems you solve, the more wealth will pour into your life. The more you serve others, the more wealth you will achieve.

3. **Organize your life to matter more to others.** The more you make your time and life valuable to those around you, the more wealth you will gain. Develop valuable skills, network with high achievers, and focus on serving people.

4. **Begin to think in terms of passive income.** If you are continually selling your time in exchange for money, then your income is limited because your time is limited.

5. **Begin to think in terms of multiple streams of income.** Don't put all of your eggs in one basket. Look at other ways to bring in resources to take the edge off and accelerate your income. Take a passion, and turn it into money.

6. **Visualize wealth.** See yourself making money. Visualize total financial abundance flowing toward you. You can tap into this vision.

7. **Cancel out negative thoughts.** Guard your thinking. If you allow garbage into your mind, you'll get garbage results. If you have great ideas, you'll get great results. Monitor your internal dialogue and what other people are saying to you, especially regarding wealth.

8. **Choose friends who have a wealthy mindset.** Who is on your contact list right now who are like-minded, progressive thinkers about money? Be with people who think and act positively toward financial freedom.

9. **Believe that a wealthy mindset is a healthy mindset.** All the roads you take are governed by your attitude. Don't have a poverty mentality. Set your mind on building and growing wealth.

Of course, there are many people, like I once was, who don't realize any of this. Not only do they lack the financial acumen, but they're short on motivation. They don't have the passion or the forward thinking to seek and implement what needs to be done to pursue their own wealth and financial freedom. Many of us are making up for our past. We may have grown up poor or lacking, and that can create craters or voids in our thinking. *I didn't get a chance to have this before, we reason, so, I am going to make up for it now.* But instead of saving our money, we spend it.

The better approach is to set a platform in front of you by creating a steppingstone for your future. You can never go back to the past and pick up things that were broken. Yet you can start to mend ways and move forward. It takes energy, and you may be so busy trying to make up for something from the past that you don't have the motivation to do something for the future. You simply can't see it. It is hard to envision, but you can create it through mental imagery and form a model for saving and investing. When someone talks about money, they talk about how much they make or how much something costs. They generally don't mention how much they invest. People say, "I make six figures," and they want to make seven figures, but what part of that are they investing for the long term? I worked for the government at NASA, so I didn't get social security from them, but people think they will live off of that when they are older. Yet social security wasn't made for living off of. It was designed to bridge gaps and make life better. It is not the end all, be all. Social security alone is impossible to live from and still have a lifestyle you desire and deserve.

A great and effective way to gain the knowledge needed to pursue financial freedom is through mentors. One of mine is my cousin, R.J. He was in the military, and he and his wife started their own company. They made $350,000 a year, and it ended up being a million dollar business. He went on to acquire a finance license in investing. He taught me things I never knew before. Another mentor, Sharon Wamble-King, was a business executive from a young age, and when I was an executive at NASA, she was an executive in an industry that created a skill set in understanding finances within her.

Charles Capps is an author of books such as *God's Creative Power for Finances* and *The Tongue, a Creative Force* who has helped me amplify the affirmations I mentioned earlier. I once talked to his daughter, Annette, who took over his ministry after he passed away. She told me a story about how her father would go to a piece of land he wanted God to give him.

"He'd say, 'Land, you belong to me. God says I am over creation and over things, and I want this land. God is going to give it to me, so you come to me now.'" Then he'd get in the car and drive away. "We would drive to that land," she told me, "and my daddy would get out and talk to that dirt. I would just laugh, my daddy kept talking to it, and I'll be, God did it." He got the land, and Annette believes in such affirmations today. Bill Winston was a mentor who wrote a book, *Revelation of Royalty*. Winston grew up thinking Christians were not supposed to have a lot because that meant they were prideful, but after I studied it, I came to believe that I am supposed to have a lot, so I can be a lot and give a lot.

Through what I've learned and experienced, I have become a mentor to women, some of whom, such as Je're Harmon and Desiree Cook, are featured in this book. My heart is to develop people, make them better, and reach into the core of their existence to pull out those things they didn't know had been planted inside of them and present it to them in a way to recalibrate their thinking. A vital aspect of that recalibration when it comes to creating and building wealth involves reverse planning. It involves introducing yourself to your future self by leapfrogging ahead so that you can smell, taste, see, and feel your desired future. Then you work back to the present and say, "Here's what I need to do. Here's what I am not doing. This is what is going to make a difference." That is followed by a gap closure plan where you make intentional decisions concerning what you want to achieve and need to obtain to get there. It gives you an analytical perspective of where you need to go.

Such plans can reveal some old habits and suggest a new direction when it comes to handling money. So many of us were taught to save when we were younger, but not to invest. Saving is short term, has more liquidity, and can help you over the next six months to a year-and-a-half depending on who you are and your risk tolerance. However, if you want to grow your financial capability, investments are a must because they allow you to earn compound interest. There is a broad list of things that you can invest in. Some do this through mutual funds, others through stocks and bonds, and others still through real estate and business and residual income where they receive passive income. However you choose to invest, it is a long-term play, ten or fifteen years out, and a key part of a harmonious, balanced portfolio for amassing wealth.

When I look at the word "balance," I think about harmony. You have to be responsible to grow wealth depending on where you are on your journey. You need to think about what is coming in, what is going out, and what is growing. If more is going out than coming in, that means you have a lack of balance, or harmony, in your finances. Growing wealth is defined by having more coming in, and more working for you, than you have going out. Such financial responsibility creates financial discipline. To maintain that harmony, it's best to diversify rather than place all your financial eggs in one basket. One thing may be growing and doing well when something else is lax and slow, so a diversified portfolio allows you to continue to grow wealth. I often see people making exquisite types of investments such as in rare art, vintage cars, or in Bitcoin or Ethereum cryptocurrency hoping that everything will pan out, but markets can be too volatile or too fluid, and it can cost you.

A great ritual that will help reinforce the value of your wealth is regularly assessing your net worth. Your net worth is the total value of your assets minus your liabilities or, more simply put, what you own minus what you owe. It's a key indicator of financial health, but hardly anyone knows it, much less evaluates it. How can you reinforce the value of wealth if you don't know your net worth? I recommend doing it quarterly. That way, you can see what you can and cannot buy and what you can do to improve your financial health. I look at what is growing and what is not growing, including pretax savings, pretax and post-tax investments, my tax exposure, insurance, and the risks I am willing to take on all of those. Another great habit is to regularly ask yourself, "How much do I currently need per month in order to live the standard of life that I want?" Then ask yourself, "How much will I need per month in

10-15 years to live the standard of life I want?" Finally, consider what you want to leave behind for the next generational line? These routines will inform and reinforce your value proposition as a person of wealth. Do the analysis. Have conversations. Make checking your financial well-being as important as it is to regularly go to the doctor.

I have identified seven simple yet dynamic steps that you can take to begin thinking and dreaming your way toward your pursuit of financial freedom. These are also from the book and workbook *Financial Healing from the Inside Out*.

1. **Think positively.** The fastest way to begin doing this is to take your mind off yourself and your problems. Start thinking about how you can help someone else.

2. **Think creatively.** Consider ways to tackle a particular situation differently. Begin thinking "outside the box" without placing conditions or limitations on what can be accomplished.

3. **Think purposefully.** Carefully assess all avenues that need to be examined, being mindful of, and making preparation for, the possibility of encountering challenging situations. In the business world, this is done through a SWOT

Analysis, where you list of all your Strengths and Weaknesses (internal factors that show where you are strong and competitive but may have limited resources) and Opportunities and Threats (external factors that indicate who and where your competitors are and how you may overcome the challenges in dealing with them).

4. **Think elevated thoughts.** Utilize your discernment to move forward and make decisions without being judgmental, self-sabotaging, or blaming others. This requires moving beyond the chit-chat going on in your head. Consider the majestic eagle. It sits perched high and has a view of the entire area beneath him. The eagle is also a master flyer. It does not needlessly expend its energy by flapping its wings but soars with wings spread wide on currents of strong thermal winds. Finally, the eagle is bold and courageous. It has no fear of engaging the enemy.

5. **Think of solutions to your problems.** Don't just sit in your problems. Listen to and observe a problem while it's in action. It's one thing to read about how a multimillionaire came up with a particular solution; it's quite another to become that multimillionaire yourself. When you can witness a problem in action, then you can utilize the gifts you already possess to define the moment when a solution is to begin.

6. **Think long-term.** Look beyond the present and ponder ahead to what will happen in the distant future and develop a strategy for sustainability. This does not mean placing something in the back of your mind with the expectation that someday you'll eventually get to it. Rather, you are to actively establish measurable goals with a clear picture in mind, outlining the definitive steps that need to be taken in order to reach each one of those goals, and how long each goal will take to fulfill.

7. **Think of possibilities and opportunities.** I get excited about opportunities associated with wealth. I get excited about potential. I operate from thinking about what the possibilities could be. That's my mindset. Yet I have other family members, including Lonnie, who are more conservative, and they keep me level and help create good decisions for everyone affected. From the standpoint of conflict, we see it as creative tension. Handled appropriately, that results in conversations, compromise, and healthy, wealthy outcomes.

For those just getting started on their journey toward financial freedom, I ask them to consider their mindset concerning wealth. I used to believe that I could amass great wealth in a short period of time, but I didn't have a plan. So, if you wish to be extremely wealthy in a short period of time and you don't have a plan, go back to the drawing board and come up with reasonable, logical steps to get your desired outcomes in a specific period of time. Next, turn those steps into specific, measurable, actionable, relevant, and time-bound goals to get there, then take those and break them down into smaller, realistic strategies to achieve those goals. Something many people overlook is whether or not their employer has a matching fund program. If it does, take advantage of it. Don't hesitate.

I view wealth from a legacy standpoint. My desire is to be a beacon of light and a place of hope for structure, discipline, possibility thinking, and optimistic pursuits. I want my kids, grandkids, and great grandkids to have the opportunity to get an education and be productive members of society. I don't want them to have to struggle or to suffer. I believe promise, prosperity, and blessing come only from God. I have what I have because He is the source I can then have as a resource for the things the next generations of my family need. In the end, values are very important. They keep you aligned with being productive, creative, innovative, and industrious so that you can make an indelible impression on the earth for God and become an influencer for the Lord. Values are the core to your being, your fiber, and your existence. They speak to who you are and what you pass on to others. Don't lose sight of who you are and who you are purposed to be. See the possibilities!

Dr. Amanda H. Goodson is a groundbreaking aerospace engineer who soared to become the first woman to hold the position of Director of Safety and Mission Assurance out of the Marshall Space Flight center at NASA. She participated in over 35 successful launches. Transformed from a young African American girl who was told by her teacher that she would not amount to much, Dr. Goodson uses her unstoppable "can do" spirit to inspire others to achieve their goals regardless of the obstacles.

Dr. Goodson is an Amazon Best Selling Author of the book: Women Leading by Faith: Make a Difference Now. She is also a published author of over 25 books and workbook. Noted nationally for her achievements, Dr. Goodson has served on the Board of Director's Chair for Advancing Minorities Interest in Engineering (AMIE), in addition to serving in leadership positions for a Fortune 500 aerospace company.

Contact Dr. Goodson at AmandaGoodson.com

CHAPTER 5

Well Done

LOVELY GANTHIER

BEING THAT I now have my own accounting firm, fortified by my passion for the principles taught and outcomes possible as a member of the Bold.Millionaire. Women + Men movement under the direction of my pastor, Dr. Amanda Goodson, it certainly makes sense that my interest in money management began as a little girl. I was inspired as I watched my parents practice their individualized concepts of wealth building.

I grew up in a home where money was both a discipline and an art form. My mother treated it like a contract with clear rules, precise steps, and absolute accountability. "Do well in school and doors will open for you," she'd say, her eyes scanning every column of grades as though she were weighing my future on a balance sheet. Receiving a B+, no matter how close to an A, could bring me to tears. Her voice, steady but firm, carried the weight of expectations that I internalized as law. I wasn't just being raised; I was being trained—trained to believe that excellence was the only acceptable outcome.

My father, on the other hand, approached money like music. He was a self-taught musician who believed that wealth was a song, a rhythm, something that flowed when you created value people couldn't resist. "If people value what you bring," he'd tell me, "they'll find a way to pay for it." He didn't measure me against test scores or report cards; he wanted to know if I was curious, if I was daring enough to improvise, if I was willing to make mistakes in search of a new sound. Where my mother saw a contract, my father saw a canvas. For him, connection and creativity were currency.

Looking back, I can see that I was being shaped by two entirely different blueprints for building wealth, one rooted in structure, predictability, and academic achievement, and the other in possibility, resourcefulness, and the courage to follow inspiration. At the time, I didn't know how rare it was to have both influences at once. But I did know I loved them both.

Even as a little girl, I was curious about the mechanics of money. I wanted to know not just what a dollar could buy but how it flowed. Why did some people seem to multiply it, when others just seemed to watch it slip through their fingers? I listened closely to the way my parents spoke about bills, savings, and opportunities. My mother's language was about security and planning. My father's was about creating and attracting. Their conversations became my first classroom.

Outside of those lessons at home, I turned to books and became an avid reader. I devoured anything I could find about personal finance, but nothing electrified me like Robert T. Kiyosaki and Sharon L. Lechter's *Rich Dad, Poor Dad* series. I was fascinated. Those books introduced me to concepts like financial independence and the difference between working for your money and having your money work for you. I wasn't just learning how to manage money, I was learning how to use it as a tool for freedom. They showed me concepts like cash flow, financial independence, and assets versus liabilities. It was in those early readings that I first encountered the idea that money could be a tool for freedom, not just survival—that financial freedom isn't about survival. It's about choice. It meant waking up in the morning and deciding how to spend your day without the pressure of a paycheck determining your options. It meant having both security and possibility. It meant saying "yes" to opportunities out of vision, not fear.

At school, my mother's influence was obvious. I worked hard, took leadership roles, earned excellent grades and collected scholarships. I joined clubs and played sports, not just because I enjoyed them, but because I had learned to see every opportunity as a steppingstone. My father's influence showed up in the way I approached challenges. When an assignment felt boring or unnecessary, I looked for a creative way to make it my own. I didn't just want to meet the requirements; I wanted to create something memorable.

The tension between perfectionism and creativity became a kind of duet in my life. On one hand, I was meticulous, double-checking everything, analyzing every detail, and refusing to turn in anything that didn't meet my high standards. On the other hand, I was drawn to big ideas and imaginative solutions. I craved innovation, freedom, and expression. Sometimes these two parts of me fought like rivals. At other times, they harmonized beautifully, creating results that were both precise and original. Do you lean more towards perfectionism or creativity? What would happen if you let them work together instead of against each other?

When I stepped into the working world, the influence of both my parents' philosophies became clear. From my mother, I had inherited a relentless drive for excellence. She had drilled into me the importance of showing up prepared, following through on commitments, and letting the quality of my work speak for me. From my father, I had inherited the courage to try something new, the instinct to seize opportunities, and the understanding that creativity wasn't a distraction from work it was an asset.

That blend made me adaptable. I could excel in structured environments, but I also knew how to step outside the lines when a situation called for it. Early in my career, this adaptability became a quiet advantage. Still, as much as that blend served me, I had one obstacle to overcome: perfectionism. The standards I held for myself were high, sometimes unreasonably so. Perfectionism whispered that nothing I produced was ever quite ready, that I needed to review it one more time, polish it a little further, hold off until it was flawless. It made me hesitant, fearful of missteps, convinced that any imperfection would disqualify me. The truth is that perfectionism brings delays that become the enemy of progress. I didn't fully understand that until I began working with mentors who challenged me to see things differently.

The turning point came when I began to seek mentors—people who could expand my vision and help me overcome my own limiting patterns. One of the first was Michel Valbrun, a seasoned certified public accountant (CPA) and entrepreneur. Michel said something that stuck with me: "Done is better than perfect." At first, I resisted. But slowly, I realized that my perfectionism was less about excellence and more about fear. Perfection was safe. Perfection meant avoiding judgment. But it also meant avoiding progress. Around that same time, I began working with Brittany Ndiaye, who taught me another truth that pushed me out of my comfort zone: "Visibility equals profitability." Marketing myself had always felt intimidating. What if I said the wrong thing? What if I looked unpolished? But Brittany helped me see that invisibility was a far greater risk. Staying hidden guaranteed I wouldn't grow.

Between Michel and Brittany, I began to learn that forward motion mattered more than flawless execution. Progress requires exposure. Growth requires risk. Perfectionism protects your ego, but progress builds your legacy. Progress requires exposure. Growth requires risk. They encouraged me to step out, even if I didn't feel ready.

I'll never forget the first time I recorded and posted a video introducing myself and my company. I was terrified. I taped words of affirmation to the wall behind the camera, reminders that I was capable, prepared, and called to do this. Even then, I had dozens of "erase and start over" moments. I stumbled, I critiqued myself, I almost gave up. But eventually, I got through it. The final video was simple: me, explaining who I was, what my company did, and why I was so passionate about helping people save money through implementing tax strategies. I posted it with trembling hands, convinced no one would watch. To my surprise, the video received over 200 views. It wasn't viral by internet standards, but to me, it felt monumental. Michel laughed and said, "You basically went viral!" Brittany cheered just as loudly. They celebrated with me as if I had just crossed a finish line. And in a way, I had. That one post broke the dam of perfectionism and showed me that courage matters more than numbers. Their words pushed me past perfectionism into visibility. That courage on camera was training for a bigger leap: to build a firm by faith, not fear.

Launching my own firm wasn't a spontaneous decision. It was the result of years of preparation, networking, and a willingness to step into the unknown. In truth, I had been practicing faith long before I could name it that way. Every risk I took, whether applying for a scholarship, seizing a new role, or stepping out of my comfort zone was faith in action. It was believing that unseen effort could produce visible results.

But there is a difference between faith in risk-taking and faith rooted in relationship. My early financial mindset came from my parents' examples and the personal finance books I devoured as a teenager. Faith was present in my life, but it was more of a background melody than the lead voice. I didn't yet understand how deeply it could shape my approach to money and business. That connection, faith not just in outcomes, but in God Himself didn't come until later. And when it did, it transformed everything. If I could risk embarrassment online, I could risk stepping into entrepreneurship. But while I had been practicing faith in risk-taking, God was about to show me what it meant to practice faith in relationship.

The turning point of my journey began at the Leaders and Volunteers Conference hosted by His Presence Church in Tucson, AZ. I went to serve, learn, and maybe make a few new connections. I never expected a moment that would reroute my life. During one session, a comedian engaged the audience with quick, lighthearted questions. I answered one, and he looked right at me, smiled and said, "You're smart; you belong over here with Dr. Goodson." His tone was playful, but I knew deep down it was more than a casual remark. It was a nudge from God, disguised as a joke.

Earlier that day I purchased ten of Dr. Goodson's books. She signed each one personally, writing inscriptions that felt less like ink on a page and more like prophecy. In one, she wrote, "I hope that God changes your life." I didn't take that lightly. I received it as a seed planted in faith, a divine agreement over my future. When she spoke at the conference, she also invested a dollar in the life of every participant. I could not bring myself to spend mine, so I invested it. Months later, what began as curiosity became commitment. I visited her church for the first time, then again, and eventually became part of the congregation.

Over time, Dr. Goodson invited me into mentorship. She refuses to let potential stay dormant. From the beginning, she spoke to the future version of me. She didn't just affirm my present; she pulled me toward my potential. "Aim higher," she said. "You are good enough to serve millionaire clients." Those words landed like an assignment. It was about stewardship, about refusing to shrink when God had entrusted me with more. It fueled me. She gave me work right away: complete a SWOT analysis of my firm and of myself. It pushed me beyond tactics into self-awareness. Under her guidance, faith moved from background melody to the lead voice. We prayed over decisions. We aligned strategy with scripture. She reminded me that stewardship is spiritual and practical, and that excellence is a form of worship. Her mentorship stretched beyond business. On days when my headaches were severe, she didn't just offer advice; she prayed with me. Not polite, surface-level prayers, but deep, powerful intercession. Through her, I learned that true leadership touches the whole person, not just their productivity.

As my firm grew, I knew I needed the right teammate. That's when Benz appeared. He arrived at his interview having researched one of our clients so thoroughly that he proposed specific recommendations before he was even hired. I saw preparation, humility, and a level of initiative that told me everything I needed to know. Bringing him on was an easy "yes." Mentoring him became a joy: watching light bulb moments as he grasped a nuance in tax code and tax law came alive as a tool for strategy or saw how a strategic shift could transform a client's outcome. We built a culture where curiosity, integrity, and service came first—and results followed. This was more than training an employee, it was multiplying a vision.

All this mentorship, prayer, and disciplined strategy sharpened the way I serve clients. Working with clients, I've seen how strategy turns fear into freedom. One woman nearly lost faith in her business after being blindsided with a $25,000 bill from the Internal Revenue Service. I can still see the slump in her shoulders as she described it, the heaviness in her voice, and the way her eyes carried both fear and fatigue. She wasn't just facing numbers; she was facing despair. We worked together to rebuild her confidence with a proactive tax plan. Slowly, the fear lifted. Strategy gave her back her hope.

Another client came to me treating her work like just a side gig, hesitant to step into her full authority. When we reframed her business as a family enterprise, she lit up. She hired her children, not only unlocking tax benefits, but instilling skills and confidence in the next generation. Her mindset shifted from hobbyist to CEO. The joy she felt overflowed into community. She even organized "coffee chats" with friends, eager to share what she had learned. Her transformation multiplied into others' lives as she suddenly saw herself as a CEO and her household as a legacy-building team. When she gathered friends to learn over coffee, she was refreshing others. It's as Proverbs 11:25 promises. Whoever refreshes others will be refreshed. Her joy multiplied as she poured out.

Then there was the client who expected a $5,000 tax refund. He had resigned himself to modest results, not realizing how much he had left on the table. When I uncovered missed deductions and credits, his refund grew to $17,000. The stunned smile on his face wasn't just about the money; it was about possibility. Strategy had shifted his reality. These stories remind me that growth is never one dimensional. It's a layering of discipline, creativity, faith, and stewardship, each building on the other.

That layering of lessons didn't begin with my career or adulthood. It traces back to moments in childhood that shaped how I saw money and responsibility. One of the most vivid comes from my time in the Bahamas, a place where life itself teaches you to think about resources differently.

The Bahamas has a rhythm that seeps into your soul: the steady pulse of waves brushing against the shore, the gentle creak of fishing boats swaying in the harbor, the sweet and salty air perfumed with bright hibiscus. Life there moved at its own pace, unhurried yet intentional. Even water carried a lesson. In our home, it didn't flow endlessly from the tap. It arrived in both gallon and five-gallon jugs, plastic containers delivered to our door, each one held with care.

Those jugs became more than water to me; they became metaphors for wealth building. I started with my very first jug, a plastic container I slowly filled with coins. At first, the sound was sharp: the clink of metal against emptiness. But as the bottom filled, the sound softened, the coins cushioned each other. That change in sound was proof of progress, verification that I could build something from nothing. I remember the smell of copper and nickel on my fingertips, the way coin paper rolls crackled open like tiny scrolls. I'd count, stack, tap the ends flat on the table and line the rolls like soldiers—pennies, nickels, dimes, quarters. On Saturdays, I'd walk them to the bank, the jar lighter in my hands, my heart heavier with accomplishment. Filling that first jug was fulfilling. It wasn't about the amount; it was about the act. Each coin was a step of discipline. That jug became my first "accounting system." I soon expanded, dedicating one jug for pennies, another for nickels, another for dimes, and another for quarters. I had a system. Pennies taught me patience. Quarters taught me acceleration.

Those rituals taught me three truths:

1. **Momentum has a sound.** It starts as a sharp clink in an empty jar and becomes a steady hush when there's a foundation.

2. **Not all inputs compound equally.** Saving pennies builds patience; saving quarters accelerates outcomes. Strategy matters.

3. **Systems create peace.** When money has a place to go, it stops running your life.

Later, when I automated transfers and built investment schedules, it felt familiar—like upgrading from a
gallon to a five-gallon jug. Same faithfulness, bigger
capacity. Even at that age, I realized strategy mattered:
the same discipline applied to different resources created
different results. Each coin in my jug was a rehearsal
for the truth of Matthew 25:23: as I was faithful over a
few things, God would make me ruler over many things.
Faithfulness with pennies was preparing me for stewardship of millions. Saving was my first strategy. What is
the first jug you need to start filling today? Is it a savings
account, a debt payoff jar, simply putting $10 aside each
week for a dream fund you've been afraid to begin?

But I learned quickly that saving alone wasn't
enough. Saving builds security, but it doesn't create
multiplication. To build legacy, you need both saving
and investing. Saving is the foundation—it teaches discipline, patience, and delayed gratification. Investing
is the expansion—it teaches vision, strategy, and the
power of compounding. The key is knowing when to do
each, and how to balance both. Have you been playing
it safe with saving alone, or are you also building for
legacy through investing?

Coins and currency taught me something else: the
importance of multiple streams. And just as I learned
to separate the coins, I learned to separate income
streams. One jug of income can only hold so much. But
multiple streams, like business revenue, investments,
real estate, even side gig opportunities create resilience.

Diversification and protection allow us to grow from gallons to wells, from wells to reservoirs. Are all your resources coming from one jug, or are you building multiple streams that protect you when one runs dry?

Currency is not just money. It's movement. It's life. Water is not meant to sit still. It is meant to move and flow freely. When it becomes trapped, it stagnates. The same is true of money. Hoarding turns abundance into scarcity. Let water flow and it creates power. Light and electricity can only be created in the flow. The flow keeps resources alive. Flow equals energy. Hoarding cuts the power. As Luke 6:38 reminds us, we are to give, and it will be given to us in a good measure, pressed down, shaken together, and running over.

We are blessed to be a blessing. I learned this lesson in a tangible way one evening when a church sister shared that she couldn't afford to attend the same conference where I had met and purchased Dr. Goodson's books. The cost was $40, and without hesitation, I offered to cover half. That night, I sent her $20 simply because I wanted her to experience what I knew would bless her life. The next morning, my phone rang. A client I feared might not pay me at all instead sent the full payment plus a $200 tip: exactly 10 times what I had given the night before. It was God's reminder that when money flows, overflow follows. I like to call such instances moments when God in Heaven winks at me.

Sometime after the conference, my sister in Christ surprised me by returning the $20. At first, I almost refused, but I realized that her giving was just as genuine as mine. Allowing her to give honored the flow and was just as important as my giving. Flow requires movement in both directions. Currency is called "currency" because it must move, like a current in a river. When we release it, we keep ourselves connected to the stream of God's provision. It is not meant to stagnate; it's meant to move carrying life, opportunity, and faith. Where could you create flow through generosity, mentorship, or even encouragement so that others are blessed and you stay connected to the current?

Here is a six-step stewardship blueprint I've called, "From Jug to River."

1. **Name your first jug.** Emergency fund? Debt paydown? Dream seed? Pick one and automate a weekly amount to the cause, even if it's $10.

2. **Separate the coins.** Create clear "buckets:" taxes, giving, operations, owner's pay, profit. Label your accounts so money knows where to go.

3. **Schedule your flow.** Twice a month, allocate percentages (not guesses). What gets scheduled gets stewarded.

4. **Add a second stream.** Monetize one skill or simplify one offering. Rivers don't rely on rain; they draw from multiple sources.

5. **Tithe time or treasure.** Pick a rhythm of generosity. Give on purpose and watch scarcity lose its grip.

6. **Review and rejoice.** Have a monthly 30-minute money meeting. What did you learn? Where did you refresh others? Where did God refresh you?

During the early days of my firm. I made a commitment: one day each week would be tithed not in money, but in service. I became a Volunteer Income Tax Assistance (VITA) volunteer. VITA is a nationwide, IRS-supported program where trained volunteers provide free tax preparation to families with low to moderate incomes, seniors, and underserved communities. The program is usually administered by local nonprofits to provide free tax preparation services. In Tucson, I partnered with United Way of Southern Arizona.

I expected to prepare a few returns. Instead, God opened the door to leadership. After passing every level of certification across all the tax areas they serve, the coordinator, Mimi, approached me. "We could really use someone with your level of expertise to run this new office," she said. That office was in the busiest zip code they served. If I hadn't stepped up, the site might never have opened.

At first, the site was quiet. People didn't yet know we were there. But as word spread, the office became a hub of activity. We grew from a handful of clients to long lines wrapping through the waiting room. Families, seniors, immigrants, single parents, all sorts of people with different backgrounds came for help. Some were nervous, others overwhelmed. But they left relieved, sometimes even smiling through tears, because someone had guided them through what felt impossible.

The gratitude we received was humbling. One client brought us baked goods to say thank you. Another left with tears of relief when she realized her refund would cover overdue bills. Another hugged me when she realized her refund would keep her lights on. I had the privilege of mentoring volunteers on my team. One young man, a community college student, grew leaps and bounds during his service. At first, he was timid, worried about making mistakes. By the end of the season, he was confidently guiding clients, asking good questions, answering questions confidently, and even helping others troubleshoot. Watching him flourish reminded me that when you pour into others, you never come out empty.

I believe all water is good. Lakes are good for relaxation. Wells are good for drawing. Rivers are good for life. Lakes collect and reflect, but rivers move and renew. Lakes can hide stagnation beneath a glassy surface, but rivers confess their direction in every ripple. A lake can provide rest and reflection, but a river creates movement, energy, and power. Electricity comes from flowing water, not still ponds.

In the same way, God's promises of multiplication are unlocked in the flow, not in hoarding. Months after tax season, I prayed for a new position. I described it to God in detail: the responsibilities, the culture, and the benefits. That very day, I opened LinkedIn and saw a posting from United Way of Tucson and Southern Arizona for a senior staff accountant. I applied and called the VITA director, who said, "You'd be great. Energy like yours is rare." The next day, while I was still in prayer, my phone buzzed with a missed call. It was United Way, inviting me to interview. When I arrived, the VITA team came out to greet me. I wasn't just another applicant to them. I was family. Seeds I had sown in service were now bearing fruit—and I got the job. I don't believe that was coincidence. I believe it was the return on every Wednesday I had given away.

We are all born with talents that enable us to contribute to the lives of others around us. Many of us profit or make money using our gifts and talents and that is absolutely acceptable but if we only use them for ourselves, we miss the opportunity to flow into an overflow. That is what it means to live like a river.

So, I challenge you: start with what you have. Pour in faithfully and let it grow. Let it flow, bless others, and watch how God multiplies it back to you. Then, when you've built your jug into a well and your well into a river, you'll hear the words that echo through eternity.

Well done.

Lovely Ganthier is a skilled accountant with expertise in tax strategy, advisory, and planning services. As the founder of Team Wright Taxes, she is dedicated to helping individuals and businesses optimize their tax savings. She also works at the University of Arizona as a Grants and Contract Administrator.

A passionate community advocate, Lovely is the author of The Cesar Clause: Strategically Cut Taxes and Build Wealth and coauthored the article Sorteando (Sorting Out) Systemic Barriers and Social Support Promoters of Women's Health in the Journal of Racial and Ethnic Health Disparities. She is deeply committed to empowering others and giving back, actively participating in multiple community initiatives. Lovely is particularly passionate about her work with I AM You 360, a nonprofit she serves on the board of, which builds tiny homes for young adults aging out of foster care and provides customized hygiene products for foster children that address their specific racial identities.

Contact Lovely at teamwrighttaxes.com

CHAPTER 6

---◇♛◇---

Even Greater

DAKEESHA WRIGHT

FROM THE TIME I was really young, it became my intentional, personal mission.

I wanted to make sure my parents did not have to pay for me to go to college.

So, when I completed high school, I had no fewer than 20 scholarships available to me, but only one was going to give me a full ride and cover all of my tuition for as long as I attended. I took it—along with additional ones to cover books and whatever else I needed.

My parents did not have to spend a dime for my education. But that wasn't all. My schooling also afforded me the opportunity to do internships every year. At age 17, only two weeks out of high school, I started my first one at an aerospace and defense company.

Twenty-eight years later, I'm still at that same company.

I earned my degree from the University of Texas at Arlington in mechanical engineering in 2003 and was hired upon graduation. From there, I utilized the company's employee scholar program to further my education and get my master's degree from National Graduate School in quality systems management in 2010.

My fierce sense of independence may not have been common back then, especially for African American females, but I've always been that way. I was gifted in math and science, so when my father asked me in ninth grade if I had ever thought about being an engineer, I naturally started looking into doing classes and activities around that, and it took off from there. My parents were divorced and had both remarried, but they provided well for me. They weren't rolling in the dough or anything, but it was never a problem. I started working at age 15.

I've always had a drive to be independent—to be and have something even greater!

That same drive has influenced how I handle my money and pursue my financial freedom. I never wanted to be in debt. Therefore, my husband, Josh, and I currently do not have any debt except for one home mortgage. We actually have two homes, our residence and a rental property. In addition, I have always been about paying off credit cards. In fact, I use them to my advantage. If I open a credit card, it is for a purpose. One of the things my dad, who often traveled for work, instilled in me was signing up for cards with benefit programs. Whether it is for travel or buying a vehicle, I get it, use it, and then pay it off. I learned that when you put an expense on many credit cards, the charge appears on the next billing cycle, and they allow you the first 30 days after the billing cycle to make a payment. That provides a little bit of time beyond the first 30 days to pay it off. The most important thing is not to spend beyond your means. I believe paying interest on something is wasting money, so I keep it in the forefront to try my best not to do that. It actually upsets me when I do pay interest on something. It takes some research, but know your billing times, and use them accordingly. Understand your credit card and how it works.

When it comes to large purchases. I enjoy luxury items, but I love coupons, too. Early in our marriage, I prioritized saving money whenever we could on most small items such as meals (I still take my lunch to work) because I'd rather use my money on nicer things that I really enjoy. I sacrifice a few things, but it doesn't seem that way because sacrifice helps me get the things I want. Then, with those luxury purchases, we look for opportunities to have reduced rates. For example, if I want to buy a watch, we wait for a deal on a credit card where the rate will go down to 1.9 or two percent. So, if we are paying interest, it is reduced, and we are able to pay it off in a shorter amount of time.

On my journey to be financially independent, I always knew there was money out there for me to go get. I remember how my mother always signed up for sweepstakes when I was young. She showed me that if she filled out the same kind of card, as soon as she got the sweepstake all she had to do was put whatever they were asking for on the card. She'd pull out a card with the information already on it and simply add to it when necessary to make it easy to fill out the forms. I used that same mentality when I pursued all those college scholarship applications. I wrote an essay that covered many of the basic questions the various applications asked, then simply adjusted it to each application depending on what else they wanted to know. It wasn't a chore. It made the process easy.

It's great when we can realize that taking care of our finances doesn't have to be hard if we put a little forethought and creativity into it. Watching the ways my father managed our family's money was how I first learned to do it myself, and I do the same thing now with my children. I joke with my six-year-old twins about how many flight miles they're going to have by the time they get to college. I tell them, "You won't have any reason to not fly home." I have tried to start having conversations with my kids as well as nieces, nephews, and younger siblings about money, just like my dad did with me. I have also learned a lot from Suze Orman. I loved watching her show on television, and she now has a podcast. I enjoy hearing the scenarios of how other people deal with certain financial situations. I have never stopped learning when it comes to money, even when it comes to items such as life insurance or making the right choices for my children to continue to thrive after I am gone. Generational wealth is exciting.

I see creating and building wealth as a multifaceted process that, done well, can shine like a sparkling diamond. It starts with the good money practices I covered earlier. Not owing a lot of money on credit cards, paying those off expeditiously, and saving money on interest are solid foundational strategies. That way, you are not living paycheck to paycheck and are able to save money as well.

To begin to significantly grow wealth, you want to first realize that it is something that you do for yourself. Your choices make it happen. My husband and I, for example, have investments in real estate property. We wanted to own, not rent and pay someone else's mortgage. It was important for us to see that benefit for ourselves, as well as for our parents. If they were not in a place to purchase, we provided for them and kept the wealth within the family. Whenever we move, which we've done quite a bit with my job, we make it a point to always purchase the home we're living in. Often, we have been fortunate to be in a market where we were able to get really good interest rates and mortgage payments significantly lower than if we had rented something equivalent. If I own, it builds wealth for myself and my future generations. I can choose to pay these homes off and provide them to my children.

We also invest. We began small, not knowing what to do or how to get into the stock market, and we read, investigated, and learned about the market. We decided to invest in real estate investment trusts, or REITs. We had several different REITs for a few years. It was a good way to invest in real estate when we were just starting out, and it showed us a different side of investment. We were able to grow our funds in that manner as well—to the point that, in May 2025, we started our own business. We feel this decision is going to take us toward real wealth. It was my brain-child, but my husband and I launched it together. It is called Melanin Minds in STEM, and it is an organiza-tion designed to look at the landscape of executives in the STEM industry and purposefully help minorities in STEM to see themselves in executive positions.

When you look across today's business landscape, the C-suite, or the body of top-level executives in a given organization, doesn't have a lot of diversity. After the directives issued by the United States' Equal Employment Opportunity Commission and subsequent executive order by President Donald Trump in March 2025, there have been fewer efforts in the U.S. to recruit and hire deserving, talented minority professionals into those higher-level seats. Melanin Minds in STEM aims to give those professionals the coaching and tools they need to compete at those levels and ultimately acquire those seats. We'd also like to connect them to current minority executives so that they can network with those who are already in the C-suite and learn success strategies from them. A lot of what I am doing is giving back to my community to develop and grow our youth, so they can succeed in STEM fields like I have as an African American female. To that end, we are committed to partnering with youth STEM organizations or attending events in those communities.

All along the way, my husband and I manage how successful we are in this business. When you are working in an organization, you are there to make the company successful, but at the end of the day, you don't hold the bottom line. With your own business, you also own the bottom line. That positions you to see success with long-term growth and significant wealth.

There are fundamental differences between saving and investing, and both can serve you well in building and managing wealth. Saving is the opportunity to take excess money that isn't already designated for some other purpose and put it into another account. These funds may or may not be gaining interest, depending on how you save them. Investing is taking money and placing it somewhere where it definitely could grow. The stock market is one way you can do this. An investment in stocks can go in either direction, so you're taking a bit of a chance, but stocks can provide an opportunity for a lot more growth than savings because percentage yields in the returns are a lot greater. You can also see day by day whether your stocks went up or down in value. However, if you invest in real estate, your return won't necessarily be as visual. Diversification in investments is great because having multiple ways to invest grows your portfolio by leaps and bounds. Not all of your investments are going to do well at the same time, so it's great to have variety in your portfolio. Finally, savings are good in that you always want to have cash readily accessible. With investments, your money isn't that accessible, and it takes a bit of work to get it back if you need it for an urgent need or emergency.

Consistent with how I view and use credit, it is clear that credit plays a huge role in building and managing wealth. Credit is usually the foundation and base to reach further heights and do more things. Therefore, your desire must be to keep your credit as pristine as possible. There may be times when the minimum is all you can pay. Since I never wanted to pay interest, I tried to avoid that as often as possible, but when I was just starting out, I didn't have the means to pay everything as I wished. So, whatever you're able to do, strive to pay in a way that will appear positively on your credit report. If you can only pay the minimum, try to pay that plus a dollar. It will show that you are making good progress. Pay every month to keep your credit in a positive light, then continue to grow. Ultimately, that'll afford you the opportunity to do the things you want to do like buying a vehicle or a home. Likewise, protecting your business credit will allow you the ability to secure lending at desired rates. The better your credit, the lower the rate. Simply put, if you are not protecting your credit, you are not able to use it wisely or in a manner that benefits you later.

To understand and manage wealth responsibly, I learn. Because I was trained in mechanical engineering, I did a lot of reading and studying. When I finished, therefore, I wasn't one to want to read more. I'd more than done my share. But my husband, the reader of the family, helped me to see the value in continuing to read about wealth. That is how we discovered a lot of our strategies. Podcasts are good, too, as well as qualified research online. In the summer of 2025, I also connected with an organization called Black Women Invest. It offers learning platforms and opportunities to partner with like-minded women who want to connect and learn about financial investment. As I progress, I have found that my desire to grow wealth and financial responsibility and my need to grow are one and the same. I want to continue. I don't want to stop. It goes back to the same drive that took me through engineering school. That curiosity, the knowing that I *can*, just fuels me to want to do more.

I don't think I will ever settle. People around me say, "I wish you would just sit down sometimes." But that same drive continues burning inside of me. It has taken me to great heights within my organization, with my new business, and personally as I build wealth and pursue financial freedom.

I have two rituals that I believe reinforce the value of wealth in my life. They may not significantly move the needle, but they certainly help my mindset. The first started when I was in my early twenties. Once I paid my bills at the end of the month, whatever I had left in the account was pushed into savings. Sometimes it wasn't much. Other times it was more. It depended on the month, but that was how I taught myself to save. The second involves my children. From the time they were born, whenever I got paid, they got paid. I placed a small amount of money, five dollars at first, into a separate account for each child. It has been impressive to see how quickly each fund has grown. Now I am starting to get into money market accounts for them. Money in those accounts cannot be touched for a certain amount of time, but it is building a literal legacy of wealth for them to have later in life.

To be sure, leaving a legacy of learning, understanding, and appreciation of money and wealth is huge. I want to leave financial opportunities for my children that maybe I didn't have. In terms of access for my future generations, I'd like it to come with some level of responsibility. Without that, I don't think it will be valued. You've likely heard people say that if someone has to purchase something themselves, they will take care of it better than if it was just given to them? That's a fact. I want to make sure my future generations are well taken care of, but if they don't understand or value the amount of effort it takes to get it, it will not be treated the way it is intended. In fact, it could be spent before you blink an eye. Josh and I want our children to carry on the legacy.

I've found that navigating the emotional aspects of wealth is tough. If I knew somebody who had done it successfully, I'd pay for their secrets. It's not easy. More money equals more problems is a true equation. Sometimes other people have a different perception of your wealth. They assume you have a lot of money just lying around. That's not necessarily the case, but they still assume what they want to. Then, if you manage your money well, you are often the person they go to when they need monetary help. You have to be ready and willing to balance your desire to support friends and family with making sure you are keeping yourself financially whole. It's an emotional journey, and I don't know if I have it down perfectly. Every day and every situation is different. My parents didn't have to do anything to help me monetarily for college, but they certainly provided well for me as I was growing up. Now, they are getting older and may need support or help in their later years. My husband and I want to make sure all is well with our parents.

For those who are just underway on your journey of financial freedom, I applaud you and encourage you to stay the course. You've just gotta start in a comfortable place. I wouldn't tell anyone to go out and invest all the savings you have, but if you can step toward something you aren't as familiar with, learn more about it, and start, that's huge! Then, as you continue to get more comfortable, you can try other things. If you have a good idea, and you want to make a difference, start your business. It could eventually turn into something that you never imagined. Start somewhere, and you'll see how it can progress into something even greater.

Dakeesha Wright is the CEO and founder of Melanin Minds in STEM, a leadership platform created to elevate minority professionals into executive roles. With a background in Engineering & 25+ years in the aerospace industry she brings lived experience, strategic insight, and a relentless commitment to making sure greatness never gets left behind. As DE&I efforts evolve, Dakeesha ensures the momentum continues — developing tomorrow's leaders through accelerated training, mentorship, and inspiration at every level, from classrooms to boardrooms.

Contact Dakeesha at
Dakeesha@melaninmindsinstem.com

CHAPTER 7

The Long Game

CHANDA ALLEN-BAFFOE

MY JOURNEY TO building wealth started at a pretty young age and involved scotch tape, envelopes, and the persistent, loving model of my parents.

I grew up in Maywood, a suburb of Chicago, Illinois. My mom, my younger sister, and I lived in a modest two-bedroom home. I'd eventually head off to college from that house. My parents divorced when I was young, but my dad, Charles, ensured his presence in our lives. My mom, Sharon, remarried when I was 14. It was absolutely a loving home. I gained another dad, Sammie, who my sister and I affectionately call Popi. To this day, he still loves us like his own. Most of my family lived in the Chicagoland area, so we gathered for every holiday. We were very close.

When I later reflected on my childhood as a young adult, I was extremely proud of my mother's strength. I keenly observed how hard she worked caring for two daughters as a single parent and as a human resource professional with International Harvester. That reinforced a sense of independence and determination to be self-sufficient. How that translated into financial independence was one of the guiding lights throughout my younger years. I followed my mother's counsel as she instilled into my life the concepts of going to school, getting good grades, going to college, and getting a good job. Grades and performance in school have always been important to me. My earliest recollection is wanting to get and maintain straight A's in first grade.

I still emulate my mother's example of being mindful about money management. She and my grandmother, Roberta, enjoyed spending Saturdays shopping at garage sales. Some of the clothes my sister and I wore were the product of those outings. We wore second-hand clothes, and even though I tried to hide that from my classmates, I can look back and see that as an important life lesson; it has contributed to my beliefs and behaviors today. I learned the opposite of materialism. It also gave me a great lesson on appreciating vs. depreciating assets and how things such as clothes and home goods depreciate. Later in life, my father, Charles, who is an attorney, would teach me some tax strategies as a small business owner. As a child, I watched him request a printed receipt for everything! He kept track of all expenses and denoted those which were related to his law practice. Today, there are tools that make this process easier.

As a 10-year-old, I started selling what we might now call movie theatre candy at school. My surrogate great-grandmother would sell it to me at a significant discount, then I would sell it at school for 100 percent profit. At 12-years-old, I started earning more money working for my cousin as a "shampoo girl" at a beauty salon. I took what I made and allocated certain amounts for various things, placing each designated fund into a different envelope and taping each envelope to its own page in my "banking" notebook. I used the tools at my disposal, so a plain spiral notebook served me well for what I would later understand was the "bucket method" of saving. One envelope was labeled "Candy." Another was earmarked as "Savings." I had as many as seven buckets in my banking notebook.

That initial process grew from there until by age 13 my mother agreed that I was ready for my own checking account. Later, as I became a young adult, I continued the journey with an unchanging mindset of investing in the present with an eye toward the future. That mentality played into some of the decisions I made concerning my career. I had a willingness to sacrifice immediate gratification with the recognition that I was building toward a stronger, more independent future. Back then, that meant self-sufficiency. Today, that is still the foundation, but it also means financial independence—being able to do what I want to do when I want to do it. My goal is to have one boss in addition to God, my seven-year-old son, Chandler. It also means giving back and building a foundation for a legacy that will last for generations.

Early on, I took advantage of opportunities to invest in savings plans. At age 19, in my first internship with Motorola, I started contributing to a 401(k), which positioned me for growth in an investment portfolio. As I increased my income, I increased my portfolio and its diversification. For example, I converted my Motorola 401(k) plan into a traditional Individual Retirement Account (IRA) when I left my internship. My mother, and a quick consultation with her financial advisor, encouraged me to do that. Upon graduation, I joined The General Electric Company (GE) and immediately began investing in a 401(k) and receiving GE's matching contribution. Years later, a friend would tell me that when she was at GE, she didn't know a 401(k) with a company match was available to her. I thought everyone knew! For me, this was confirmation that there is still a great need for financial awareness. Not everyone is aware, especially first-generation college students or those descending from marginalized groups. Sacrificial willingness was not enough; being exposed to saving and investing options was critical. I'd initially gained this exposure from my mother.

The bucket approach which began in my youth certainly helped me build wealth as an adult. Today, my journey continues in parallel with my role as an executive at an aircraft engine manufacturing company where I have served for over a decade after spending nearly 15 years with GE. By education, I am an electrical engineer. But by heart, I am a servant leader. This service leadership was germinated early with initial exposure to mandatory service projects in high school. I now serve on the board of Cool Girls, an organization that supports growth and development in the community and focuses on giving girls exposure to help change their world and, ultimately, ours. It provides mentors, scholarships, after school programs, and workshops. I have also served on the Local School Council in my county, tutored elementary and high school students, and am an avid mentor. I now reside in Georgia after first living in the Peach State back in 2002 and then South Africa and Connecticut in between.

Because of my lifelong perspective of building wealth, I know that it takes time. There simply aren't too many people who are overnight millionaires or billionaires. It may seem that way on the outside, but we don't always see the work it takes for those individuals to arrive at that achievement. Whether the approach is aggressive, conservative, or something in the middle, building wealth is a long-term process that requires patience and wisdom, at least for the majority who do not experience things such as instant fame or large inheritances. As an investor, I understand that the stock market will fluctuate. We must not be afraid to set aside money to invest for the future. I started with an envelope savings method, moved to a bank-based savings account, and then on to a 401(k). Subsequently, I created a brokerage account that allowed me to buy and sell stocks, bonds, mutual funds, and other assets. I continued to grow my portfolio and diversify my investments to include REITs (Real Estate Investment Trusts), community bonds, and real estate along the way. Because I recognized the importance of appreciating assets, I did not rent long after college and bought my first home at the age of 25. Today, I would advise people to make that purchase even sooner if feasible. For example, investing in a college home or domicile that enables a rental space is a great introduction to business and asset building for the responsible college student. As parents, even finding ways for your pre-collegiate children to support you in your investment endeavors can instill great lessons at an early age.

In order to have available funds to invest, I had to recognize that my inflow should exceed my outflow. As I continued to grow my inflow or income, I did not increase my outflow at the same rate. Now that I have a family, I serve as the budget "boss." It all started with the correct mindset. I accepted that budgeting and allocating for the future was a requirement, not an option. My philosophy and approach revolve around the concept of "pay yourself first." As I've progressed through my career and grown in position and resources, I have maintained that philosophy and practice, increasing it to scale according to where I am at that moment. Though my expenses increased, so did my saving habits and more exponentially. In other words, the more I made, the more I spent, but the more I saved, too.

Some people might characterize all of that as "living below your means," but I don't feel like I am sacrificing or missing out on anything. I like to invest. I also enjoy seeing my money grow and my assets appreciate. I recognize that it is very difficult to delay gratification. I look around and see people enjoying the full spoils of their labor. Even as an engineering student in college, I observed others whose studies may not have been as rigorous as mine go off and enjoy themselves a little bit more than I did. Sometimes, those who delay gratification may get discouraged by what we see around us. After all, the future is not promised. Yet when I look back after more than two decades, I see that it certainly has been worth it. Selective delays of gratification or sacrifice also build discipline. As I've done the work and adjusted along the way, I've seen my money grow. Understanding what motivates us is also critical. Part of my motivation stemmed from wanting to be independent, self-sufficient, and give back. Once my godchildren and, much later, my son, were born, my motivation for making each generation better than the last grew exponentially in meaning.

I can't adequately express how important it was to learn how to manage my money as a young girl. However, when I went to open my first checking account, I came up against an obstacle. Officials at the bank thought I was too young for the responsibility. There was no law. There was nothing written that indicated that I could not have a checking account at that age, but back then I was breaking new ground. There weren't too many 14-year-olds coming into financial institutions requesting to open a checking account with the full support of a parent saying, "She can do it." In the end, my mother's support was the key. The bank required her to be a co-owner of the account, and she agreed, but insisted that her name not appear on the checks. My name, and mine alone, was there, and my money, and mine alone, went into that account.

To this day, I have never bounced a check. That's a testimony to the confidence and discipline potential that my mother saw in me. She knew that I was a good steward of money. I'd proven I had enough discipline, even at that age, to step into areas that some adults struggle to manage. I was initially issued a temporary checkbook where I had to write in my name and account information, but when that first box of fully printed checks with my name on them arrived in the mail, I was so excited! It was literal proof of the sense of discipline and accountability that I had developed, and it would be a steppingstone for my growth in personal financial management and literacy.

During my upbringing, my mom emphasized "go to school, get good grades, and get a good job." The assumption was that if I got that good job, I'd be able to thrive in life. My view was that it would generate income, build wealth, and I would gain financial independence. I concluded that I'd always had that drive and discipline as a youngster by observing how hard my mother worked and reinforced it. Through the example of my parents and others around me (sometimes of what not to do), I recognized my own desire to be self-sufficient, and I automatically equated the ability to be independent with having money or wealth. At that time, I believed that the more wealth or financial independence I could acquire, the more I got to make my own decisions in life.

I laugh now when I hear my son say, "I wish I were an adult, so I could make my own decisions." I think, You have no idea how many people I must answer to as an adult. Today, financial independence means something different to me, but I am grateful I held that perspective as a child. It motivated me to set a foundation where I didn't feel like I needed to keep up with everyone else. While the lesson of my youth, "go to school, get good grades, and get a good job" has served me well, I am positioning my legacy to change the narrative for my son and the next generations. Yes, go to school and get good grades—but then build businesses and a career you are passionate about. Elevate communities by generating opportunities for others; creating jobs, not just "getting one." Ultimately, support yourself and the next generation by building wealth.

God entrusts us with a little, and if we prove faithful with that little, God entrusts us with more. Had I proven back then to be unfaithful with that little, I don't know if

I would be in the right place for the "more" that I have right now. In fact, today I would define financial independence as being positioned to follow my passion without the concern for how I generate an income as a principal focus. Most people consider retirement age as 62 or 65. I plan to have that ability well before that age, and it is due to much of what I previously mentioned: how I've approached budgeting, money management, striving for growth and progression, investing and making trade-offs.

Have there been setbacks in my journey? We had our house broken into in 2014. A lot of things were taken, and that was a period of significant discouragement. However, I struggle to call it a setback because, if anything, it made me more determined—extremely angry and hurt, but insistent on moving forward. I have dealt with significant losses including the loss of my sister to cancer and a significant mentor to a heart attack. I've seen other colleagues who also died earlier than expected. Those jolting events make me more conscious of balancing living for today while I plan and save for tomorrow. I've faced each situation and turned them into opportunities to grow, develop, learn, and overcome. It is a great mindset to acquire and nurture.

The Bible mentions being equally yoked with your partner, united with someone who shares the same faith and values to work toward shared goals. I am a little more of a stickler than Kwame when it comes to finances, but we are lockstep on our overall careers, values, and wealth aspirations. During our wedding vows over 20 years ago, I said "I take you, Kwame, to be my lawfully-wedded husband, to have and to hold from this day forward, for better or for worse, for richer or for RICHER—which we will build together." I spoke financial life into our marriage. My God, my parents, and my circumstances motivated and spoke financial life into me. Together, I am very proud of what my husband and I have built, and we continue to build upon this with our son. We speak accomplishments, wealth, and financial independence into him and we want him to recognize that he can build upon it even further.

Having mentors and mentees has helped me focus as a professional and as a changemaker dedicated to building wealth, securing my financial freedom and that of future generations. As I think about the guidance I've received over my life and career, I must recognize my "board of directors." These are individuals who know me and can provide coaching and honest feedback much like mentors do. It is not enough to hold up a mirror for reflection through a corporate lens only. I need people who have lived with me, known me since childhood, and seen me through other pivotal phases of life who can shine a light on the whole person and illuminate how I show up in different arenas. That helps me remain centered and aware of my journey, not just where I am at a given moment. This board also serves as advisors, sponsors, and listeners, and it consists of professional mentors, career coaches, family members, and even mentees. My board is less about positions and corporate titles and more about lived experiences, authentic interactions, and their ability to provide perspectives that stem from sincerity and a genuine interest in my well-being. Sometimes this means they share hard truths and tough love, yet every one of them has an experience from which I can learn. My board also includes my parents and my husband; talk about those who will provide hard truths and tough love. They shine the light on elements of my journey that have shaped who I am today, my personality, and my aspirations.

The mentor who passed away was someone I worked with professionally. He believed in me and challenged me to stretch and grow in the corporate arena. His candid feedback and stellar professional and knowledgeable example helped me in ways for which I will be eternally grateful. Whether it was debriefing meetings together that could have gone better or ensuring that my voice was heard and presence felt in the room, I knew that I had his support. He was also a sponsor who spoke up for me in rooms that I was not in or able to speak for myself.

Mentors can also be significant sponsors aiding our success and growth. Sometimes mentors and sponsors are different people. It is important to understand the role of each "board member" in your life and how these individuals can reflect various aspects of you in different environments. I have a mentor who did not start off as one. Our roles led us to interact periodically over the course of several years, and he challenged me at every turn. A board member encouraged understanding, so instead of running the other way, I continued to seek connection, understanding, and alignment. I ensured that we met quarterly, and occasionally I would take a meeting we had in common from his office. This created space for candid feedback, not only for me, but for my team. He has become a mentor and someone that I can reach out to for perspective. He will contact me with feedback he believes is important for me to hear. We have built a strong rapport and trust that makes him comfortable to do this, knowing I will manage that information appropriately. A coach, outside of my professional realm, is one who certainly holds up a mirror for me. She saw that while I was an achiever, I was chasing instead of allowing things to come to me. It was a powerful reflection, and her input provides perspectives on what I want to accomplish, who I need to help, my "why," and when I simply just need to be still.

I recognize that I am a rarity: a black female engineer and Fortune 500 company executive. I don't take that lightly. I appreciate how others elect me as a member of their own "board of directors" to serve as an advisor in their journeys. Sometimes I coach, by asking questions and allowing them to contemplate and arrive at their own answers. Other times, I mentor, providing my perspective and experiences and what I learned along my journey. There are also opportunities to leverage relationships and create new connections for them. Most of my individual mentees are within my current industry, but I also advise students and other industry professionals.

Helping others progress toward their goals as either a mentor or a coach is a significant "why" for me. The ability to leverage my experiences to help others means that I am making a positive difference in their journey. One mentee was in a role that was not favorable for him. I was able to put him in contact with a couple of leaders in different organizations. Those connections resulted in a new role better suited for him. His career perspective changed significantly, as did his expectations and environment. That excited me! Another gentleman, who had been with the company much longer than I, was promoted after I connected him with one of my mentors. In the process, I helped him understand that he not only had to focus on executing his job but also on managing his career. For him, the key was being intentional about his career moves, sharing his aspirations, then engaging others to be accountability partners invested in his success. He is now positioned to allow his skill set to shine while being more aware of how to navigate the corporate landscape. I continue to mentor him today, and the gratitude he expresses about changing his whole trajectory, perspective, and approach to his career means I am making a difference. In both examples, it is really inspiring to know that I had a hand in impacting someone's life and seeing that shift. It makes me think about others that I can impact and what more I can do to make a difference that extends beyond myself and my lifetime!

For anyone starting out, these five strategies offer an effective foundation for creating and growing wealth. First is saving for compound interest. With compound interest, you not only earn interest on the initial amount deposited (the principal), but also on the interest that accumulates over time. This has an exponential effect on your balance. The longer the money is in the account and compounding, the faster it grows. It's like a snowball effect.

Second is delayed gratification, which references establishing the discipline to go without something today (not a "need" but a "want") to build for the future. I delayed the gratification of excessive partying as an undergraduate in college so that I could get my engineering degree. That degree was a building block for my career and wealth building and has paid itself off many times over. Simply giving up three specialty drinks a week at your favorite coffee shop and placing the money you would have spent into a high yield, interest bearing account can make a difference. That money can be used later to take an international trip, pay for a child's first semester at college, or even treat yourself to a bigger "want." Delayed gratification is a valuable discipline that can be applied to other areas of life.

Next is understanding appreciating versus depreciating assets. An appreciating asset is one that grows in value, such as a house, stocks, bonds, rare art, and fine jewelry. A depreciating asset is one that bears its highest value at the time of purchase, such as a car, shoes, and most clothing.

Fourth, look for ways to save money. No matter how much I make, I still clip coupons and look for sales and bargains. Why spend more money unnecessarily? I'd rather use it for experiences, including luxuries that I enjoy such as travel. Paying yourself first doesn't mean just scrimping and scraping. Treat yourself kindly. That makes saving worth it, and it continues to serve as a reminder of a future worthy of excitement and anticipation.

Lastly, diversify your investments. I began with a savings account. I am an interest-earning chaser. I'll occasionally scour banks to see who has the best interest rates, and I will open an account with one if I see that they offer a significantly better interest rate to cash incentive. I'll then utilize that account for some of my liquid holdings. Money under a mattress or in a bank that is earning little to no interest doesn't work for me. The more I work for my money, the more I want it to work for me. The essential difference between investing and saving comes down to risk and assets. Saving allows you to put money in accounts that are fairly secure. Depending on the type of account, it may or may not earn interest. Investing, however, allows you to place money into assets that have the potential to appreciate and increase exponentially.

There are certainly differing levels of risk when it comes to investing. Real estate, or property, is an example of an appreciating asset typically. Money placed into a home or a business is done with the anticipation that sometime in the future that entity will be worth more than it is worth today, providing a strong return on investment (ROI). The idea of investing is to spend money now with the intention that it will gain value. When investing in stocks or the stock market in general, those who are long term investors want to put their money in companies that they believe have a secure future and will continue to grow or make money incrementally year after year. I fall into this category, although day traders and those who short the market (bet against companies) can experience significant financial gains as well.

It is important to diversify your investments because everything has a cycle. There was a period when the real estate market and property values hit a low. The money that was spent on real estate in 2008 was likely under the value one would have normally paid (buyers' market) while 2021 proved favorable for the sellers who commanded top prices for their properties, and receiving more than asking was not unusual in many parts of the United States. Yet when housing was at a low, there were certain stocks, like technology stocks, that were appreciating significantly. When housing prices were peaking in 2021, there were companies on the stock exchange struggling due to the existing pandemic. If you put all your money in one place, it can drive decisions that may not be best for the long term and can have larger impacts on your net worth and overall financial health. In the earlier example, if you had money in both technology and real estate, you could weather the one that was struggling because the other was thriving.

I have an insatiable curiosity and joy toward understanding and managing wealth responsibly. I love it, so I study it, but it doesn't feel like work. The more I talk to people about money and managing personal finances, the more excited I get. It is a passion for me. In early 2025, I went to a business workshop that taught attendees how to properly establish an LLC, structure a business, and be mindful of tax laws and advantages. There was even someone there who spoke about life insurance. I began deepening my understanding about the different types of insurance coverages available. I would leave that workshop and dig deeper into the life insurance arena to learn more. Fundamentally, the more I learn, the more I want to know and the more I share. It is exciting!

I encourage those who may be intimidated by the idea of learning about finance and wealth, or who perhaps are even fearful thinking about what they have and what they don't have, to start small. Make a commitment to do one thing differently. There are savings accounts and money market accounts available where you can earn three or four percent on your money. From there you can take a little bit out and invest in a stock, bond, or a mutual fund made up of a bunch of stocks across different industries. Then, when you get your next merit increase, a raise, or a tax refund, put it into an interest-bearing account or an investment account. You can utilize that money as it grows to invest in other assets. It is really one step at a time.

Don't allow perfection to be the enemy of good. A lot of people say, "I don't have a lot, so I can't—" You can, even with a little. If you make $100, save one dollar or 50 cents. Just start somewhere. If you don't feel as disciplined with money management or don't trust yourself with it, there is so much technology today, people available to support, and different techniques and tools you can use to help.

A great motivator for building wealth and achieving financial freedom, in addition to self-care, is the legacy you can leave behind for future generations. My desire is to leave behind appreciating assets, instruments that my son can use to improve his life and build upon our legacy. I also want to leave assets that organizations we donate to can utilize to improve the lives of others and change their trajectory to impact generations. Building financial and physical assets that surpass my lifetime is critical to how I define success. I also want to be a beacon of education and information so that people know how they can grow wealth for themselves, then go and teach others. I love the timeless proverb that declares (paraphrased), "Give a person a fish, and you feed them for a day. Teach a person to fish, and you feed them for a lifetime."

Chanda Allen-Baffoe is a powerhouse of purpose, passion, and performance—with over 25 years of global corporate experience and a track record that spans industries, continents, boardrooms, and black belts (both the Six Sigma and martial arts kind!). She has served in numerous senior and executive leadership roles across the Medical, Energy, and Aerospace & Defense sectors.

Chanda is a graduate of esteemed programs including the McKinsey Black Executive Leadership Program and the General Electric Operations Management Leadership Program. She earned her Bachelor of Science in Electrical Engineering from the University of Illinois at Urbana-Champaign, an MPA from Georgia State University, and a graduate certificate from the University of Virginia – Darden School of Business.

Recognized as one of the Top 50 Women Leaders of Connecticut by Women We Admire in 2023 and

2024, Chanda is also a proud member of United Way's Tocqueville Society, an active career and personal finance mentor, and a board member for Cool Girls, Inc. When she's not leading billion-dollar programs or inspiring the next generation of changemakers, Chanda is out exploring the world—having visited over 50 countries and all seven continents, and spending time with her amazing husband, Kwame, and their charismatic son, Chandler.

Contact Chanda at budgetboss.ab@gmail.com

CHAPTER 8

Risky Business

MARVIN CAROLINA JR.

I AM A huge risk taker.

Therefore, I'm a big believer in the adage, "Don't be afraid of risk."

In the time I've spent going back and forth between entrepreneurship and corporate America, I have taken risks. I've stepped out in faith, and I've done well. But I've also had some stumbles along the way. Obstacles have popped up, and things haven't gone great all the time.

But I can tell you this. The risks have been more than worth it, especially because they have positioned me to be able to generate wealth and pursue financial freedom.

Education is the basis of my achievements. I have a strong foundation, beginning with a great high school and continuing through my pursuit of an industrial management

137

degree at the Georgia Institute of Technology and later, a master's degree in community development from North Park University. I continued learning and growing into my early career in sales and leadership at Oscar Mayer and Kraft Foods, Carolina Beverage Distributing, and Sears, and education certainly remained the backbone of my 15 years of service as vice president of diversity at J.E. Dunn Construction. As president and CEO of the Better Business Bureau of Greater Kansas City and in my work as a public speaker, trainer, and consultant, I maintain that focus on education for myself, my clients, and the constituents I serve. I've been blessed to work for some great corporations in wonderful positions, as well as branch out as an entrepreneur.

Risk came into play all along the way as I took some chances, did well, failed, jumped back in, and did it all over again. That is my story, and I had fun with it along the way. The first time I really stepped out and risked it all came when I was living in Los Angeles, California, doing exceptionally well in corporate America working for Oscar Meyer and Kraft, and I decided I wanted to be on my own as an entrepreneur. Nothing bad was going on. My job wasn't high pressure. I wasn't working with people I didn't like. I enjoyed what I was doing at Oscar Meyer and Kraft—but I was at a tipping point. I wanted to do something different and exciting, knowing that if it didn't work, I could come back to corporate America. It was a combination of restlessness and curiosity that told me, "Come on, let's go do something!"

So, I did. I returned to Georgia and went back to school. I didn't have a plan. I didn't have a strategy. I really had no idea what I was doing—which is not at all something I would suggest to anyone today, but that was my path then, and looking back at it now, I'm proud of it. I spent a few months searching for opportunities until I found the one that interested me: distributing bottled water. I got a truck and gained the rights to distribute Grayson Bottled Water, and I started building from there. I began by selling water to workout facilities, small gas stations, restaurants, and magazine stores located on the first floor of high-rise buildings throughout Atlanta, Georgia. The business started growing, and I hired my first driver. Everything was going great.

But my mistake was that I didn't raise my prices as expenses increased. My profit margin shrunk as my expenses grew. In addition, the drivers I used did not have a sales mentality. There is a huge difference between a delivery person and a salesperson. So, when my drivers walked into a place that was not that big and were instructed to market, sell, and leave 20 cases of water, that didn't make sense to them, so they'd only sell and deliver five cases. I'd have to go back to sell the balance. That's when my growth slowed, and before I knew it, I was out of business.

That experience taught me the value of better understanding all aspects of my business, especially human resources and how that affects the financial side of the operation. As an entrepreneur, everything from sales and marketing to technology and customer service was my responsibility, and I realized I had to up my game when it came to that foundational focus of education. It also hit home the fact that entrepreneurs have to understand how to manage the enterprise's finances. I don't like the nuts and bolts of it all, the debits and credits, the profit and margin. That's not the sexy part of business to me. I'm the sales and marketing guy. I'm the risk taker, and I see managing finances as more risk averse. But they were things I needed to be aware of, and I wasn't. It is critically important to ask yourself some key questions. How do I invest for my business? How do I invest for my retirement? How do I invest for my kids? They're huge.

The entrepreneurial journey continued, as did the risks. In 2004, I went into the real estate business buying homes. I went to the bank and got a loan to purchase my first investment home, and then I cash flowed it, fixing it up and renting it out so that I could buy the next one. It started well, and I had the money, but I lacked the skill set needed to succeed long term. I was paying full price for an electrician or for new drywall instead of acquiring the ability to do that myself or hiring someone who could do it all. That ate up my profit. My son, Ellis, later earned a degree in construction management field supervision, and he works for a construction company. I sure could have used someone like him then. It would have been a totally different ball game. When the whole housing market went down in 2008, it hit me financially, but I was still working at J.E.

Dunn, so it didn't take me down. I had a balance. I didn't go all in on it. If I had been all in, I would have gone under. Anyone going into an entrepreneurial venture should not spread themselves too thin, but they have to understand where they are, too.

After the real estate venture ended, I continued in corporate America, but I also began speaking, training, and consulting. I never left corporate again. It provides my financial foundation even as I continue to coach and mentor people on the side to help them reach their dreams. The coaching and mentoring I do are the manifestations of my entrepreneurial efforts, and they also help me build a legacy of helping others. It is not always about business, so I don't know if that is really a true entrepreneurial venture or a legacy building venture. I don't even charge everybody, but if I see an avenue to help them with what I know, I'll do it. As of early 2025, I had become a full-time college professor at the University of Missouri-Kansas City, teaching business. I am impacting the lives of young people as well as repeatedly traveling to Cape Town, South Africa over the summer for about two weeks. I began doing this in 2023, and when I'm there, I teach business and entrepreneurship at the University of the Western Cape, also known as UWC. It is a joy!

Throughout my journey of risk and reward, I have been building wealth as an emerging millionaire. From the very start, it has been first and foremost about putting something away, investing just a little bit of what I make along the way. My advice is to begin early and be consistent. When you get income, save or invest it one way or another. Do that every time. That's the key. Most companies offer a 401(k) or some kind of investment program. Most companies have some sort of retirement program. It is shocking how many people don't take advantage of these opportunities. Some say they can't afford to give up five or ten percent of their salary, but when they're older, they will wish they had. Believe me, I get it. Life happens. You have kids. You have to pay for daycare. My kids are a year apart, and they were both in daycare at the same time. Do you know how expensive that is? It is crazy, and once you do the math on that, taking anything out of your pay to invest can make you cringe. The literal cost of living goes on and on, and it can give you a headache just thinking about all the expenses and the debt that often comes with making those expenses.

But you can't pay attention to all of that. You just have to keep saving, saving, saving and investing, investing, investing. Whether you do it yourself or your employer does it for you, I suggest adopting a mentality that says, "I never had it to begin with, so I am going to live with what I have." That way, it is already done. This is what's left over after saving and investing, so this is what I have to work with from there.

Saving and investing may seem like the biggest risk of all, but it's one that you have to take. I have lost so much money along the way, but I have been very fortunate and blessed to be able to recover from the setbacks.

Mentorship has been an important aspect of my journey. I believe mentorship is all about people. Whether I'm a mentor, a mentee, or whatever the categorization, I just want to help others succeed. In many ways, mentorship begins as we observe people. No one is necessarily telling us, "You have to do this." We watch others, and we mimic their behavior. My father, Marvin, Sr., and my grandfather, Charles, were not very talkative people. Both of them were pretty laid-back guys. But they led by example. Their behavior demonstrated it.

When I was a kid, my mother, Jeannette, would drop me off to hang around with my grandfather. He was retired, and throughout the day we'd drive around, pick up friends from church or elsewhere, and take them to doctor's appointments or to the grocery store. I saw how he'd get out of the car, open their door, and let them go in. He'd always ask, "Do you want me to come in with you, or are you okay?" After a while, I started doing the same thing, jumping out of the car and running around to see if they wanted me to come in with them. That's where my desire to help others started.

When I look at creating and building wealth, it's nice to say that you can save and then invest, but you also have to find jobs or entrepreneurial ventures that pay a certain amount of income. If you have a job where you don't make a lot of money, you can save five or seven percent, but it is going to be hard to get to a bigger number down the road. Yes, the money grows. You invest it. You make compound interest. But you need to figure out how to grow it. Do side hustles, and find ways to make more income on the jobs with raises and promotions. The adage is true: "More money in, more money out."

To do that and more, build a strategy, and make sure you have financial professionals to help you understand that strategy. Different people have different strategies for investing their money for the long term. Do you have a good strategy for doing your taxes? Can you save a few extra thousand dollars that you can put back for investment? Tax and financial advisors are two critical people, and they don't cost that much. A tax person only charges a small fee, and a financial advisor makes their money off of your investments.

However you proceed, don't be out there just doing your own thing. Investments allow me to build generational wealth for my children. I have a trust and a will. I have some annuities that will pay an income after retirement. Then, as a tool in wealth management, I see credit as a means to an end. Don't be afraid of it, but don't let it get you into too much trouble. Big purchases of a house or car where you finance debt are good. It's credit cards that create the problem, and you have to keep them under control. Your credit card debt should be something you can pay off within a year.

I don't have to balance desire and need in growing my wealth and financial responsibility because my investments and everything are already taken out of my income. That means that I can do whatever I want with everything left over. I like to enjoy life. I don't need to make an impulsive decision to go to Bermuda or Hawaii because the money to grow my wealth is already set aside and is in place, and the rest is what I have to play with. My mother passed away when she was 68, and she and my father didn't get a chance to do a lot of the things they planned to do. I'm not going to do that. I don't want to wait until retirement. You could save everything and just live on the porch, but as I often say, the Brink's truck is not following the hearse to the cemetery. I'm going to enjoy life today.

A couple of things to keep in mind regarding investing and saving begin with the difference between the two. Savings is simply putting your money away, typically into a savings account. There is no strategy involved. You earn a very minimal amount of interest, between two and three percent. There is no real loss to it. Investing is all about growing your money. You have to develop a strategy around where you are placing your money and how you want it to grow.

This is where the second thing comes in: diversification. How are you setting up for the long term? Do you want to have an annuity that pays you when you reach the age of 65, or something that pays you income for life? What is your lifestyle, and what are your plans for using money to live out that lifestyle? Do you have a way to pay for long-term health care if needed? The answers to all of these questions will inform your investment strategy. You can break your money up to receive a few thousand dollars a month in steady income, along with your social security. You can have a 401(k) that is either conservative or aggressive in its goals and risk. Whatever you choose, I recommend constant investing using at least 15 percent of your income. The way I look at it, I do not want to be broke in old age.

For me, there are no emotional considerations, such as family dynamics and the potential for conflicts to arise, when it comes to building wealth. I have a plan, and I stick to it. I work it out with my wife, and it is our plan. We decide what we want to do with our money and our earnings, and we include what we believe is the right thing to do for our immediate or extended family members. It is not everybody's money. They are our earnings, so we determine what we will do with them.

If you have not yet begun building wealth, start saving now. That's the first step. Put away a minimum of 10 percent and forget about it. Then raise the percentage each year: 12 percent, then 14 percent, and so on. Assuming your employer has the option, set aside the minimum amount your company matches. After that, begin doing some outside things. Get a financial advisor to help you to do something simple using a few hundred dollars a month. Start growing and learn from there. It isn't complicated, and the earlier you start, the better. The more you can put away in your twenties, the more impact it will have in your sixties.

It is all about time. That is the trick to it. The quicker you can get in, the more you will win—and don't worry about waiting until you feel comfortable. You'll never feel comfortable. Some people think they can't afford to start building wealth, but the truth is, you can't afford not to begin.

Overall, I want my legacy to be one where I made a difference in the lives of others—but specifically with money, I want to create something for the next generation of my family. I want to impart knowledge about money as much as to leave them in a good financial situation. If I don't do that, the money I provide them will be gone within a year. With knowledge, they will take the money I left them, invest it, and it will stay in play for the generation after that. It's perpetual. That is the key—and that is why my entire family meets someplace special every year to visit and talk about finances. I work with them on any hurdles they have. We talk about investments and education. I have two children, a niece, and another young man who I consider to be a son. They all come to the annual family meeting. It allows us to stay together as a unit.

I also expose them to different things to help them understand something other than just the corner of the world they live in. My youngest is going with my wife and I to Cape Town, South Africa in 2025. It's incredible—and just one of the byproducts of my willingness to embrace risk and reap its rewards.

Marvin Carolina has spent his life working towards one main goal: to help others and make a difference in this world. He is a motivator, speaker, and change-maker who concentrates on areas such as diversity, inclusion, and self-perseverance. Through his years of experience in multiple industries and fields, Marvin has curated the material he needs to share powerful and meaningful stories with others to spark change. Marvin has been a part of various organizations, such as the Better Business Bureau, where he was an integral part in growing their sales and memberships, and JE Dunn Construction, where he was a significant contributor to creating their national award-winning DEI program.

Throughout his working experiences, Marvin has earned many recognitions such as the Ace Award, Community Champion, Top 40 in Their 40s Business and Community Leader, Top Contractors for Diversity (Kansas City), Innovation Award (Houston), NAACP award, and Hispanic Community Builder Award (Atlanta). Marvin's motivation to help people reach their best selves and achieve their personal and professional goals has only grown. He now finds himself providing coaching, education, and workshops to those looking to become more than they could imagine.

Contact Marvin at MarvinCarolina.com

Thank you very much for reading Thriving: Making Bold Moves. We have published several other anthologies compiled by Dr. Amanda Goodson and her team on a variety of topics including mentorship and leadership. If you are interested in writing your own book or in being on the author team of a future anthology book, please contact us at amandagoodsonglobal@gmail.com